THE Great NORTHWEST Nature FACTBOOK

A Guide to the Region's Remarkable Animals, Plants, & Natural Features

Ann Saling

WESTWINDS PRESS™

I dedicate this book to Harriet Bullitt, who published my first article on Northwest nature in Pacific Search *magazine, and opened my eyes and heart to the special beauty and diversity of this unique region.*

Library of Congress Cataloging-in-Publication Data:

Saling, Ann
    The great Northwest nature factbook / by Ann Saling.—Rev. 2nd ed.
        p.   cm.
    Includes bibliographical references (p.   ) and index.
    ISBN 0-88240-514-4
    1. Natural history—Northwest, Pacific.   I. Title.
QH104.5.N6S25   1999
508.795—dc21
                                          98–30917
                                              CIP

WESTWINDS PRESS™
An imprint of Graphic Arts Center Publishing Company
P.O. Box 10306, Portland, Oregon 97296-0306, 503-226-2402

President/Publisher: Charles M. Hopkins
Editorial Staff: Douglas A. Pfeiffer, Ellen Harkins Wheat, Timothy W. Frew, Diana S. Eilers, Jean Andrews, Alicia I. Paulson, Deborah J. Loop, Joanna M. Goebel
Production Staff: Richard L. Owsiany, Susan Dupere
Designer: Constance Bollen, cb graphics
Illustrator: Joyce Bergen
Map Artist: Gray Mouse Graphics

Printed on acid-free recycled paper in the United States of America

CONTENTS

ACKNOWLEDGMENTS

I thank the following people for help they gave me as I gathered information for this book. I assume responsibility for any errors and omissions.

Professionals include Clark MacAlpine (Friday Harbor Whale Museum, whales), Ron Jameson (U.S. Geological Survey, sea otters), Seattle Public Library Quick Information Center, Carolyn Driedger Mastin and Pat Pringle (glaciers), Roland Anderson (Seattle Aquarium fish biologist, marine life—and a belated thank-you for help with the first edition), Ed Bowlby (Olympic National Marine Sanctuary, sea otters), professors Richard Morrill and William Beyers (islands), Derek Booth (ice ages), Sally Lider (Edmonds Beach ranger, tide pools), Robert Pfeifer (Fish and Wildlife biologist, salmon and trout), Mick Wilson (U.S. Forest Service supervisor, tree insects), Ken Retallic (Idaho nature author and former outdoor editor for *Idaho Falls Register,* Idaho forests, glaciers, etc.), Dave Pehling (Washington State University Extension Service, wild bees), Karen Runkel (Oregon Tourism Department, Oregon information), and Steve Negry (Washington Department of Fish & Wildlife, bald eagles).

I thank copy editor Kris Fulsaas for patient, persistent, perceptive editing. Son Rick Saling and friend Marian Gramman helped with early cutting and rewriting. Edmonds poet-friend Joan Swift lent books, marine maps, encouragement, and Internet research. And longtime friends Rod and Eileen Cook advised about Puget Island, Portland, and silver thaws.

A special thank you to my longtime husband, Fred, who encouraged me when I thought I couldn't do it.

Mount Constitution
San Juan Islands
Lime Kiln Point State Park
Whidbey Island
Mount Baker
North Cascades National Park
BRITISH COLUMBIA
97
20
Skagit River
Lake Chelan
Grand Coule
Columbia River
Olympic National Park
Hoh Rain Forest
Mount Olympus
Ginkgo Petrified Forest State Park
Steamboat Rock
101
5
2
2
Dry Falls and Coulees
SEATTLE
90
Hood Canal
Soap Lake
WASHINGTON
90
OLYMPIA
Mount Rainier
82
Long Island
Willapa Bay
Mima Mounds
12
82
Columbia River
Snake Ri
Pacific Ocean
5
30
Mount Adams
Mount St. Helens
97
Columbia River
Wallula
30
84
N
Sauvie Island
Multnomah Falls
101
PORTLAND
Blue Mountains
Mount Hood
26
97
Erratic State Park
SALEM
John Day Fossil Beds National Monument
Sea Lion Caves
Darlingtonia Wayside State Park
20
OREGON
Oregon Dunes State Park
101
5
26
Crater Lake National Park
97
Newberry Crater
20
Malheur National Wildlife Refuge
Oregon Caves National Monument
Klamath Lakes National Wildlife Refuge
Hart Mountain
Steens Mountain
CALIFORNIA

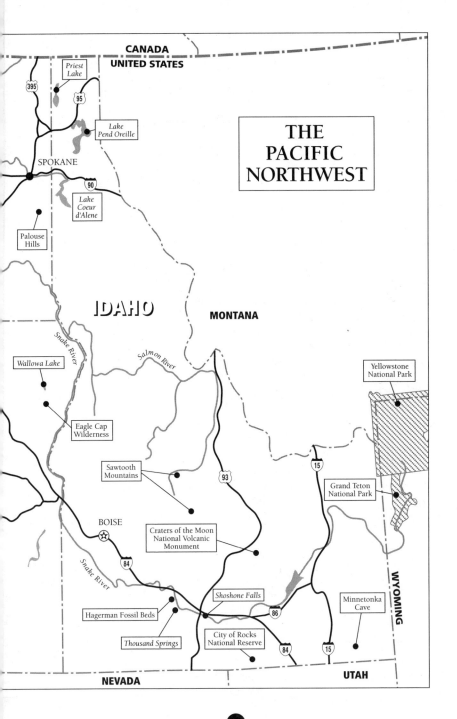

THE
PACIFIC
NORTHWEST

THE NORTHWEST

It was always the mountains I missed most during our year of Navy duty in Brasília. Our house in Seattle would soon draw us back to those mountain-filled vistas. Meanwhile, I dreamed of that snow- and ice-encrusted pantheon of Cascade mountain gods. We had traveled every possible weekend to every possible Northwest mountain to camp, ski, hike, pick berries, and photograph the incomparable scenery. I hope to evoke for you the spirit of this region, which I longed for while living in Brazil, and also in Chile, so rich in lakes, volcanoes, and simpática people—like the Northwest.

Of course the Pacific Northwest—Washington, Oregon, and Idaho— has many attractions: surging rivers with their headwaters in those grand mountains; soaring old-growth conifers (which reach their maximum size and vigor within sight of the Olympic Mountains and rain forest); animal species such as Roosevelt elk, mountain goat, and cougar, all at home in high mountains; thousands of alpine lakes, reflecting mountains in their pristine waters; and an extensive sagebrush shrub-steppe, presided over by lizards, rattlesnakes, and, of course, mountains.

The Great Northwest Nature Factbook, however, is more than a description of our glorious mountains: It presents an inclusive view of this unusual and sometimes contradictory region called the Pacific Northwest. Because the highest mountains cast a rain shadow, they directly affect the weather of the three Pacific Northwest states, creating dramatically different environments. Live on the west side of the Cascades if you don't mind being drizzled on; live on the arid east side if you love a sunny summer and a snowy winter. But there are similarities among the three states—flowers and animals choosing habitat by altitude, not by state boundary; lava and water following the tilt of the land, in whichever state they travel.

The book has three sections—animals, plants, and natural features. Each is further subdivided into distinct categories; within these, the entries are arranged alphabetically. This book is not a field guide to animals and plants, not a history book or an encyclopedic collection of facts—it is a compendium of the most fascinating and quintessential facets of the Pacific Northwest, intended to inform and entertain.

Each geographic province in the states of Washington, Oregon, and Idaho has its remarkable animals, plants, and natural features. Among the Northwest's geographic provinces are the Olympic Peninsula, the Puget–Willamette Trough, the Cascades, the Okanogan Highlands and Columbia Basin, the Coast Range, the basin and range province (also known as the Great Basin), the Klamath and Blue Mountains, and the High Lava Plains.

These diverse regions share at least one characteristic: towering mountains. From Idaho's Sawtooths to Washington's North Cascades to Oregon's Wallowa Mountains, the Pacific Northwest is defined by its mountains. Native American myths tell of godlike mountains containing evil spirits that can turn a beautiful peak like Mount St. Helens into a fire-spewing terror. And, indeed, many of the Northwest's peaks are "fire mountains." That's part of the excitement of living in this piece of paradise, the Pacific Northwest.

A N I M A L S

ANIMALS

The Pacific Northwest's enormous range of habitat—from glacial ice to marine waters, from pungent sagebrush plains to mountains so high that their uppermost zone is arctic-alpine—is home to an equally diverse range of wildlife.

The states of Washington, Oregon, and Idaho are known for their forests that, whether eastside or westside, are alike in offering habitat for animals small and large, from chattering squirrels to stately deer, from inch-long ice worms to 6-ton orcas.

The wildest, shyest animals—the lynx, the cougar, and the mountain goat—still have wild places in which to live: the many wilderness areas of the Northwest. Idaho alone provides more than 4 million wilderness acres. Its Frank Church–River of No Return Wilderness is the largest in the Lower 48; through its 2.3 million acres runs the Wild and Scenic–designated Middle Fork of the Salmon River. Oregon preserves habitat for wild animals in 35 wilderness areas, and Washington in 30.

National parks also provide protection for Northwest wildlife. Washington contains three: Olympic, North Cascades, and Mount Rainier. Oregon has Crater Lake National Park. Even at Idaho's seemingly lifeless Craters of the Moon National Volcanic Monument, many species have been sighted: 48 mammals, 148 birds, one amphibian (the western toad), and 2,000 insects.

Many animal species can be seen in the wild, from birds nesting and rearing young to residents of tide pools to spawning salmon returning to inland waters. Even in winter, animal life abounds in the Pacific Northwest. Many species migrate through the Northwest—birds on the Pacific Flyway, gray whales along the coasts of Washington and Oregon, bald eagles wintering on the Skagit River.

Every season, the Pacific Northwest pulses with animal life, from basin and range to sandy or rocky beaches to old-growth forests. Habitat is our link to birds, mammals, reptiles, amphibians, and invertebrates. The newest conservation concept, "restoration of habitat," gives hope that there will be wild animals in the future of the Pacific Northwest.

BALD EAGLE

You needn't be eagle-eyed to identify the bald eagle (*Haliaeetus leucocephalus*), with its hawk's beak, fierce eyes, strong, sharp talons, and brilliant white head and tail feathers.

The female, larger than the male as in most birds-of-prey species, stands 3 feet tall, weighs 10 to 15 pounds, and flaunts a wingspan of nearly 8 feet—the largest bird of prey in theNorthwest. The head and tail of a young bald eagle turn white only after it reaches 5 to 7 years of age.

Eagles can be observed in the Northwest most months of the year; some are wintering transients from Alaska and British Columbia, others are year-round residents. Several hundred eagles (peaking at 500) congregate annually at Washington's Skagit River Bald Eagle Natural Area, one of the four most significant bald eagle wintering spots in the Lower 48. The eagle's primary food at the Skagit River is spawned-out chum salmon carcasses.

Oregon and California share the largest group of wintering bald eagles in the Lower 48—600 to 1,000—in the Klamath Basin complex of six national wildlife refuges. In

> **The female bald eagle stands 3 feet tall, weighs 10 to 15 pounds, and flaunts a wingspan of nearly 8 feet.**
>
> ●

Oregon's Bear Valley, as many as 600 eagles roost in a single night, lured by thousands of wildfowl. Idaho's several hundred bald eagles winter near Wolf Lodge Bay on Lake Coeur d'Alene, with many nesting at the South Fork of the Snake River.

The birds build the largest nests in the world, 200 feet high in broken-top trees. One record nest was 9 1/2 feet across and 20 feet deep, and weighed 2 tons. Eagles fiercely defend their nesting territory. Bald eagles nest on the Olympic Peninsula, San Juan Islands, and even within the city limits of Portland and Seattle. Actively used nests in this area total 14 to 39.

Bald eagles actively hunt for food only a few hours a day. Saving energy, the opportunistic bald eagle often settles for wounded waterfowl, winter-killed deer or elk, another eagle's meal, or even roadkill. In the air an eagle may harass an osprey into dropping a freshly caught

fish. Few birds will attack a bald eagle. (See Raptor Havens; Comeback Kids)

CANADA GOOSE

Honk if you love Canada geese. Common in the Northwest, the Canada goose (*Branta canadensis*) with gray body and black head and throat, dramatically slashed with a white chin strap, rests and feeds in the Pacific Northwest on its way to Mexico. Normally migrants, some of the handsome geese have begun staying year-round. They or the honkers are attracted by the grass at wildlife refuges, city parks, and golf courses. Their droppings create a slippery nuisance. Never far from water, they eat aquatic plants, grass, grain, and small aquatic animals at ponds, lakes, rivers, and fresh- and saltwater marshes both in interior valleys and along the Pacific coast.

The gander, whose wingspread may reach 5 feet, stands 48 inches high and can, when provoked,

knock down a man. It guards its ground nest, and spends more than half the year helping teach

Canada Goose

survival skills to its young. Courtship and mating rituals are elaborate for the stately birds, which mate for life. (See Fly Away Home)

CHICKADEES

The black-capped chickadee (*Parus atricapillus*) can be easily identified by its song: It sings its name over and over, *chick-a-dee-dee-dee*. You can identify it also by its solid black cap and throat, separated by white cheeks above a gray back and buff sides. Fond of suet and peanut butter, it is often seen at bird feeders on both sides of the Cascades. Aggressive birds may chase it off but it usually returns. Its natural diet in summer consists of seeds, wild berries, and insects. Small flocks of the birds hunt for spider eggs, cocoons, and dormant insects under bark. A dozen birds may share a territory, establishing a pecking order with certain members driving others from a food source or favored roost.

Extremely hardy, the chickadee ranges to the northern limits of forest growth. Although chickadees will settle down in a birdhouse, pairs work together to make a nest, often lining a woodpecker hole in a dead stump with moss, plant down, or fur and feathers. To ward off predators, females emit snakelike hissings.

The look-alike Rocky Mountain chickadee (*P. gambeli*) prefers coniferous mountain forests, ranging up to 12,000 feet. In winter

• RAPTOR HAVENS •

Southwestern Idaho celebrates a raptor rendezvous each spring. Along an 81-mile stretch of the Snake River, set aside as the Snake River Birds of Prey National Conservation Area, some 800 pairs of 15 species of raptors arrive to mate and nest, more than nest in any other area of equal size in North America. The birds ascend on thermal updrafts to feeding grounds at the top of predator-free 700-foot basalt cliffs. The fine-textured, wind-deposited soil allows the growth of whitesage, sagebrush, and bunchgrass that both feed and shelter lizards, snakes, kangaroo rats, rabbits, and ground squirrels.

Species include bald eagles, rough-legged hawks, osprey, and peregrine falcons; the 200 nesting pairs of prairie falcons comprise much of the nation's total population. Summer sizzles at 100°F, but by then nestlings are fledged and gone.

Washington's San Juan Island hosts one of the Northwest's greatest concentrations of resident and migrant birds of prey, including goshawks, dusky horned owls, Cooper's hawk, and many breeding bald eagles. They profit from a lack of large mammal predators, a relatively dry climate caused by the Olympic rain shadow, a small human population, a mix of open land for hunting and wooded land for nesting, and easily caught prey: a huge population of once-tame Belgian and Flemish giant hares.

Peregrine Falcon

Cape Flattery at the Olympic Peninsula's northeastern tip ranks as the largest-known hawk migration site in North America, both for numbers of species and of birds. The Yakima River Canyon Preserve protects Washington's densest colony of nesting birds of prey. Twenty-two species of raptors are attracted by steep basalt cliffs rearing up 2,000 feet above the river. (See Bald Eagle; Peregrine Falcon) it descends to join small flocks of its black-capped cousins in stands of willow and cottonwood.

DUCKS

Ducks dine differently, depending on species: Some dive, others dabble, and a few perch. The toes of diving ducks are longer and the webs broader to help them move underwater. The stout, heavy bill aids underwater foraging.

Dabblers feed on the surface, upending in shallow water. They forage far up onshore, walking well with legs centered under their bodies, eating grass, insects, and small aquatic life. Dabblers taking flight leap from the water.

Perching ducks—freshwater birds that prefer open woodland and streams, spend more time in trees than most other ducks, dodging among branches, nesting in cavities and snags.

The common merganser (Mergus merganser) is a diving duck with saw-edged mandibles and a slender, spikelike, hooked red bill to help it catch small fish. This permanent Northwest resident feeds in open water. The skillful swimmer and diver pursues its prey underwater, using powerful feet. Its greenish crested head tops a black body with white wings and apricot breast. The young, reared in ground nest or tree cavity, are beautifully marked.

Mallards (Anas platyrhynchos), like all dabblers, prefer plant matter, but will take crustaceans and mollusks in salt water. Easily identified by the male's glossy green head, mallards are the most familiar of wild ducks, ancestors of most domestic ducks. Abundant year-round, thousands gather along Puget Sound and on bays such as Dungeness and Sequim. The male, monogamous like all wild ducks, helps guard the ground or tree nest. The mother escorts her newly hatched brood to the nearest water.

The handsome wood duck (Aix sponsa), a percher, flaunts a brilliantly iridescent black head, speckled breast, long swept-back crest, white swirls on body and face with pale yellow touches, and red eyes. Its call is a distinctive whistle. Found on both sides of the Cascades and west of the Rockies, the ducks congregate in eastern Washington along the Little Spokane River and in Turnbull and Lake Lenore National Wildlife Refuges. It often nests in snags and tree cavities on lower Columbia River islands. (See Fly Away Home)

> **Perching ducks spend more time in trees than most other ducks.**
>
> ●

GREAT BLUE HERON

Infinite patience in stalking prey, graceful flight, and elegant plumage characterize the great blue heron (Ardea herodias). A familiar sight in shallow waters west of the Cascades, the long-billed, long-necked, long-legged heron stands over 4 feet tall, second in height among North American birds only to the greater sandhill crane. It boasts a wingspan of 6 feet.

The great blue heron is a permanent resident of coastal areas and on lakes and rivers west of the Cascades. A subspecies lives inland. The Portland area has so many that the city has honored the blue heron as its official city bird. In nesting season, nearly 1,000 herons live in river basins and wetlands within 3 to 5 miles of downtown Portland. One of the greatest concentrations in Washington is at the margins of Grays Harbor.

The shy birds are solitary except when breeding and nesting, when hundreds may congregate. The male's dramatic breeding plumage features a black crest that contrasts with longer white plumes accenting the lower throat and breast. The upper neck and body are slate blue. During courtship the male holds the plumes erect and stretches out his neck, bending his legs as he exchanges nest material with the female. High in the trees the haphazardly built nests contain just enough twigs to keep the eggs and young from falling through.

Although a strong flyer, the heron is primarily a wading bird, a stealthy stalker of rivers, lakes, and marshland, able to adjust from salt water to fresh. It strikes suddenly with its yellow, rapierlike bill, catapulting the entire body forward. It seldom misses except when very young, but it may underestimate the size or length of a fish and choke on it. Crayfish are a favorite food, but the opportunistic feeder takes dragonfly nymphs, frogs, and rodents from nearby fields.

LOONS

The loon gives voice to the most complex, prolonged, and haunting cry of any bird. Anatomically, loons rate as one of the more primitive birds, evolved 50 million years ago. Ice-age loon fossils closely resemble today's bird. Loons are one of only a few bird species that divide their time between salt water and freshwater. Normally the common loon nests on northern inland lakes and rests or winters on salt water, including Puget Sound, the San Juan Islands, and Hood Canal, with some flying as far south as the mouth of the Columbia and off the Oregon coast at Yaquina Head.

Its winter, saltwater plumage is drab gray, with white cheeks, throat, and underparts. The spectacular white-on-black plumage with white necklace and checkerboarded back comes with spring breeding. From February to mid-June, it is flightless, changing to summer plumage.

The Northwest wintering group includes members of the two largest species, both just under 3 feet long: the yellow-billed loon (*Gavia adamsii*) and the common loon or great Northern diver (*G. immer*). Common loons also winter in Idaho at American Falls Reservoir and off the Oregon coast.

Unlike most flying birds which have light, hollow bones, the loon has solid bones that aid diving. The heavy loon—8 to 12 pounds—is poorly adapted for both land and air travel. Even when taking flight, most loon species almost run on the surface of the lake for about 100 yards. Once aloft, it flies strongly, though without grace, up to 60 miles an hour; underwater, the loon is one of the best swimmers of all birds. The loon can submerge without a ripple for an underwater stay that lasts from 1 to 5 minutes.

Only the common loon breeds as far south as the Pacific Northwest. The loon builds its nest of moss, grass, and floating debris only a foot or two from water, preferring a rocky islet protected from predators. Only a few hours after hatching, the young take to the water, learning the skills of catching and killing fish and crayfish.

MARBLED MURRELET

The Mystery of the Marbled Murrelet: Where does it nest? Although adult murrelets (*Brachyramphus marmoratus*), a seabird species whose numbers are declining, were often seen as winter residents of waters along Washington's Strait of Juan de Fuca, the San Juan Islands, and Puget Sound, for decades the birds kept their nests secret. Then, in 1989, biologists found a marbled murrelet chick dead, on the forest floor in Washington's Darrington district—far inland for a seabird.

An intensive search for nests in Oregon and Washington began. The dark-crowned murrelets, one of the two smallest common alcids, were known to fly inland in pairs at the end of the day in nesting season, with fish in their bills, and to return the next morning

Audubon gave the western meadowlark (*Sturnella neglecta neglecta*) the species name *neglecta* because he felt the bird deserved more attention.

Oregon's state bird, its yellow breast marked with a black V with white patches on each side of the short, wide tail, perches on a fence post or roof to sing bubbling, flutelike phrases with 7 to 10 notes. The female chooses her mate by his call.

This bird often nests in depressions in open grassland, weaving the tops of grass blades together for a domed roof. Common in interior valleys and arid uplands among sagebrush and basalt, most fly south or west of the Cascades for winter.

Meadowlark

Washington's state bird, the goldfinch (*Sinus tristis*), sets its biological clock by the thistle. The splendidly yellow male, only 6 inches tall, with jet black tail and wings and a jaunty black cap, arrives with his olive-yellow mate. But while other species build nests and lay eggs, the goldfinch flies about feeding on dandelion and wild sunflower seeds.

Goldfinch

In July and August, when lavender-flowered thistles bloom, each pair weaves a cup-shaped nest of plant fibers, with thistles providing a down lining and swaddling for the young, and thistle seeds ripening exactly when needed to feed the young.

Idaho's state bird, the 6-inch-tall mountain bluebird (*Sialia currucoides*), purplish blue with a whitish belly, swoops through the sky or hovers with rapidly beating wings. Its sweet warble with clear, short phrases sounds only until sunup in meadows as high as 10,000 feet.

Arriving in the Northwest as early as March, the bluebird prepares a loose cup-nest of stems and fine roots in abandoned woodpecker holes, natural tree cavities, or birdhouses. Although it prefers high, open country, the bluebird summers in lowlands to mountains, swamps to arid country. Since bitter weather kills dawdlers, the birds fly south in the fall.

Mountain Bluebird

to their seabird sanctuary. But no one had found their nests.

Then in 1990 wildlife researchers finally found five nests in Oregon and Washington. Located 20 to 26 miles inland, 100 to 140 feet high in old-growth western hemlock and Douglas fir forest, the nests, each holding a single chick, were simply depressions in the deep cushions of moss and lichens that cover the limbs of old-growth trees. Flying at speeds of up to 60 miles an hour, the parents made a round trip of 50 miles to feed their chicks in the safety of the forest. Mystery solved.

The chicks quickly gain weight on their protein diet, and as soon as they can fly, they follow their parents to the sea and the crowded island seabird sanctuaries. There the chicks learn to swim underwater and to catch small, schooling fish in open water, estuaries, and sheltered bays.

In 1992 the U.S. Fish and Wildlife Service listed the birds as threatened; any occupied nest and its buffer zone are to be protected. (See Sanctuaries at Sea)

NORTHERN SPOTTED OWL

Silent as an owl" was not inspired by the northern spotted owl (*Strix occidentalis caurina*). This well-publicized symbol of old-growth forests displays a repertoire of 13 different sounds, including a distinctive, high-pitched hoot and a series of three or four *hoos* that resemble the bark of a small dog. The low-pitched owl voice may sound like human coughs or hysterical laughter.

Owls such as the northern spotted owl that hunt in dark dense forests are much more vocal than those in open habitats. During its highly vocal mating rituals, it calls out often to stay in touch. The northern spotted owl maintains its territory and tree-cavity nest for life—5 to 13 years.

In 1905 near Lake Washington, the northern spotted owl was first identified in Washington, but little was known about it until 1968 when more than 2,000 pairs were discovered in an old-growth forest. Each pair needs about 2,800 acres of old-growth habitat. The Northwest may host more than 3,000 pairs.

The dense canopy of old-growth forest is essential to protect the young owls, which lack flight feathers for their first summer and must hunt prey on the forest floor. The birds also need mature trees with their huge canopies for shelter from rain and wind; since adults' feathers are not waterproof, the bird can quickly become soaked and cold.

Fifth-largest among North America's 19 owl species, the adult measures up to 16 to

Northern Spotted Owl

19 inches long with a 45-inch wingspan. An "earless" owl, lacking ear tufts, it sports brown feathers sprinkled with white spots, and unusual dark brown eyes. Although an owl's vision is 35 to 100 times more sensitive to light than that of humans, the northern spotted owl is believed to hunt almost entirely by sound. The slightest rustling pinpoints the position of the prey. The owl's soft feathers and a loose fringe at the leading edge of its wings silence its flight and guarantee a kill. (See Diets to Die For)

OSPREY

Imagine virtual reality that lets you fly with the osprey (*Pandion baliaetus*) on a hunt for fish. Glide above rivers, lakes, and reservoirs, watching for a shadow or movement in the water. Hover briefly at 80 to 100 feet before beginning a high-speed, controlled dive. Nearing the water, feel the osprey pulling its wings high overhead and

thrusting forward its flared legs and talons, unsheathed at the last minute. Talons and breast strike the water with a great splash at 70 feet a second and the osprey submerges to 3 feet deep, then quickly heads skyward again, its talons deep in a fish. The osprey, the only raptor in North America that dives into the water after fish, is the sole bird of prey to feed only on fish. The sharp-eyed bird has eyesight six times as powerful as human vision.

Fall and spring migrants, ospreys are summer residents throughout much of the Northwest, including Washington's Hood Canal, the Strait of Juan de Fuca, Spokane, and the San Juan Islands. Oregon hosts one of the largest concentrations of nesting ospreys in the Lower 48, at Crane Prairie Reservoir Osprey Management Area in Deschutes National Forest. The reservoir killed a forest of lodgepole pines, leaving many nesting snags near the water, where rainbow trout grow to more than 5 pounds—ideal osprey country. When those snags rotted, rangers erected artificial poles with platforms for the huge nests, 3 feet deep and 5 feet across.

Weighing only 3 pounds, this strong flier with a 6-foot wingspan can carry a trout of 2 or 3 pounds. Its flexible feet, with very long talons, are equipped with a reversible outer toe with intermeshing spines

• SANCTUARIES AT SEA •

Imagine the din of 60,000 seabirds on Washington's Protection Island. Once threatened by development, the rugged island, 1 1/2 miles offshore in the Strait of Juan de Fuca, became a national wildlife refuge in 1988. With no ground predators to molest eggs and chicks, 30 bird species breed and nest there. The rest of the year they spend quietly in the open ocean. Two-thirds of the breeding seabird population of Puget Sound and the Strait of Juan de Fuca gather there: pigeon guillemots, long-necked cormorants, black oyster-catchers, the state's largest glaucous-winged gull colony, 64 percent of its tufted puffins, and 17,000 rhinoceros auklets burrowing into the sandy cliffs— one of the world's largest breeding populations.

The birds compete fiercely for nesting sites and food, most of them raising their young on narrow ledges of 300-foot-high cliffs. The common murre lays pear-shaped eggs that roll only in a tight circle.

Many of the same species find protection on Destruction Island off the Washington coast. At peak nesting season, a million seabirds may raise their young on the 870 rocks, reefs, and islands in the 100-mile-long stretch of Washington Islands Wilderness Area.

Three Arch Rocks National Wildlife Refuge near Oceanside, Oregon, ranks as one of the largest seabird sanctuaries in North America, with 15 acres and three major rocks 300 feet high. Some 66 percent of the West Coast population of murres south of Alaska breed there. At Oregon's Yaquina Head, 24,000 breeding seabirds crowd the rocks. (See Marbled Murrelet) that help the bird lock onto a slippery catch. The osprey's only natural enemy, the bald eagle, may cause the osprey to drop a fish by striking the fish with clenched feet and then snaring it in midair.

Ospreys court with an aerial dance much like that of eagles, screaming as they soar and circle in intricate maneuvers. Paired for life, they return each year to the same untidy nest.

PEREGRINE FALCON

The most highly skilled flyer of all birds, the peregrine falcon (*Falco peregrinus*) performs spectacular aerial acrobatics that are especially impressive during territorial displays. Its normal level flight is a speedy 60 miles an hour; it is the fastest of all birds in a dive from great heights. Aided by long, pointed wings, it dives at a 48-degree angle at more than 275 miles per hour. Docile and quite easy to train, peregrines are prized by falconers.

The falcon, 20 inches high with a wingspread of 25 to 40 inches, was one of the first birds to reveal DDT's eggshell-thinning horrors. Thanks to a breed-and-release program, the peregrine has come back from the brink of extinction, its population healthy again. It is only one of many bird species that nest and rear young in Idaho's Snake River Canyon. Feeding almost exclusively on small to medium-sized birds, it prefers to kill on the wing—even birds twice its weight. It is adapted for pursuit in the open. Sharp talons sink into the prey, and the deeply hooked beak, toothed and notched, tears at the flesh. Wherever crowds of small migrating shorebirds congregate, the peregrine appears.

This highly evolved and streamlined bird of prey is large enough to kill game birds. Raptors have the keenest avian eyesight, and the peregrine tops the list with eyesight twice as sharp as the golden eagle's, and eight times as acute as human sight. Flying at 3,500 feet, it can spot a pigeon more than 5 miles away.

The mere sight of a falcon inspires terror in other birds. In 1997 a falconer with two trained peregrine falcons was hired at Spokane's Fairchild Air Force Base to frighten off the many birds, including some endangered species, that cause plane damage and human deaths when they are sucked into aircraft engines. When flocks of birds saw the falcons in the sky, they at once turned away, leaving both plane and endangered birds safe. (See Raptor Havens; Comeback Kids; Fly Away Home)

PILEATED WOODPECKER

It sounds like someone hammering in the woods. The pileated woodpecker (*Dryocapus pileatus*) drums on branches carefully chosen for resonance, announcing its territory or willingness to mate. If you're unsure it's a woodpecker you're

hearing, the pileated's harsh *kik-kik-kikkik* call confirms its presence. The nation's largest woodpecker, 16 to 19½ inches, hammers out the largest holes in Pacific Northwest trees. Since this "primary excavator" drills out a

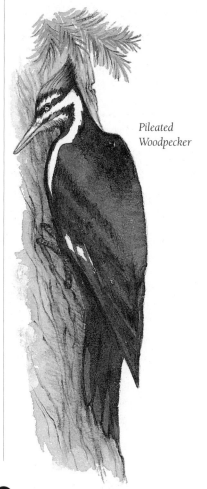

Pileated Woodpecker

• FLY AWAY HOME •

Picture the Pacific Flyway not as a sky-based freeway but as a chain of wetlands stretching from Alaska to the tropics. Migrating birds seek bogs, marshes, ponds, and estuaries for resting and feeding. South of Alaska's Copper River, however, few coastal wetlands or large rivers drain into the sea. Thus, the Northwest's bountiful wetlands and estuaries are vital to migrating birds, especially those in the Puget lowlands, the first rest-and-feed stopover for birds headed south for warmer winter habitat, and the last for those bound for Far North summer feeding grounds.

Although Washington and Oregon wetlands continue to diminish, migrating birds arrive each year in stupendous numbers. Grays Harbor National Wildlife Refuge, Washington, ranks as one of the five most vital shorebird resting and feeding areas in the western hemisphere. In mid-April, 24 bird species gather by the hundreds of thousands in the northeastern corner of Grays Harbor estuary, in 500-acre Bowerman Basin National Wildlife Refuge (NWR). The basin supports half the shorebird population while occupying only 2 percent of the intertidal land. It provides maximum feeding time, as the last area to be flooded by the incoming tide, and the first to emerge as the tide ebbs.

Almost the entire world's population of western sandpipers—more than a million—touch down at Grays Harbor. The birds relish a small, abundant, shrimplike crustacean. A staggered schedule of arrival and specialized feeding adaptations lessen competition. Shorter-billed birds feed on organisms close to the top of the mud, while longer-billed birds probe more deeply.

Some birds favor inland stops, feeding on the huge numbers of brine insects living in alkaline waters of the arid interior. The wetlands of Idaho's Grays Lake NWR attract thousands of ducks and geese, along with more than 200 pairs of nesting sandhill cranes.

Oregon's Klamath Basin is one of the most heavily used refuge systems on the Pacific Flyway, with five national wildlife refuges hosting one of the world's most spectacular concentrations of waterfowl—nearly a million at peak fall migration—including snow geese, ducks, cormorants, egrets, great blue herons, pelicans, and sandhill cranes. Lower Klamath National Wildlife Refuge, the nation's first refuge for migrating ➤

new nesting tunnel each year, the solitary woodpecker can provide homes for other woodland citizens such as owls, flying squirrels, bats, chipmunks, and five species of ducks. Those holes are unusually large ovals or rectangles, easily enlarged and quickly taken over for nesting by other animals, for whom a secure home is as important as a good source of food.

The bird wears elegant black with white underwings, flaming red crest and mustache, and white-striped face and neck. All of northern Idaho hosts the pileated woodpecker and so do many forests east and west of the Cascades in Oregon and Washington.

Forest lovers in the Northwest should be grateful for the crested bird with its strong, sharply pointed bill. Not a migrator, it excavates tree trunks for grubs and larvae all winter long, chipping and digging, cleaning out insects that can kill trees. The pileated woodpecker not only

• FLY AWAY HOME *cont.* •

waterfowl (1908), straddles the Oregon–California border, providing small marshes, open water, and grassy uplands.

Malheur NWR, also set aside as a waterfowl sanctuary in 1908, is located in southeastern Oregon's remote high-desert country. It ranks as one of the most extensive and diverse wetland complexes; 300 miles of waterways support more than 300 bird species. Malheur Lake, 20 miles long but less than 6 feet deep, receives its water from snowmelt from fault-block Steens Mountain in Oregon's basin and range province. Malheur offers one of the few natural freshwater marshes left in the western United States. Several thousand greater sandhill cranes return each year to breed. Adjacent Blitzen Valley attracts more than 250 pairs of greater sandhill cranes, noted for their incomparable mating dance. In late summer as the marshes begin to dry up, shorebirds appear, with the inevitable raptors.

speeds the decomposition of dead wood and snags, it also helps heal infested, living trees by devouring the grubs that could eat the heart out of the tree over the winter.

Basically a tree-climber, although it flies strongly, the woodpecker clings with strong clawed feet, using its stiff tail feathers for support. Listening for movement, it may chisel under bark and tear off sheets of it, or pound its bill into the wood at 13 miles an hour, absorbing the shock with its hard skull. Its long tongue, covered with mucus and backward-facing barbs, picks up insects like flypaper or shoots out to snare beetles and grubs.

A pair of pileateds ideally occupies a territory of 320 acres of dense forest, with 45 large snags.

BADGER

Never badger a badger. The feisty animal will charge a porcupine, cougar, bull, horse, even rattlesnake, biting off its venomous head. Confining a badger (*Taxidea taxus*) is almost impossible; it can chew through wood 1 inch thick, tear through pickup truck canopies, dig up uncured concrete, and break welded metal bars.

The badger abounds in sagebrush and grassland prairies in arid southern Idaho and eastern and southern Oregon, wherever small prey are present. It ranges from timberline down to deserts. North America's densest concentration of badgers digs in

Badger

the soft volcanic soil of Idaho's Snake River Birds of Prey National Conservation Area. Some 10 to 15 badgers a square mile compete with raptors for the area's many rodents, reptiles, amphibians, fish, crayfish, insects, and ground-nesting birds and their eggs. Many of Washington's badgers, especially in the southeast, were killed when coyotes were poisoned.

The badger is an extraordinary digger. Its massive neck and shoulder muscles help it disappear 8 to 10 feet into the ground within seconds, using its strong, short legs, long, curved foreclaws, and shovel-like, webbed hind feet. It also may dig with its strong jaws. This fierce member of the weasel family is second only to the grizzly in digging ability; it may scoop out a new sleeping hole every day, in addition to napping burrows. In its search for food, it tears up or honeycombs many square yards of earth, digging out rodents. Flat-bodied, only

9 inches off the ground, it easily penetrates burrows.

Few animals can match the badger's ferocity or get a good grip on its thick, loose skin. Often the badger (at 25 pounds) outweighs its opponent. An angry badger will hiss, grunt, yap, and squeal. When in danger, the stocky animal bristles, appearing twice its size. When two male badgers fight, snarling and hissing, both can end up dead, jaws locked together. The badger and its fellow mustelid, the weasel, share the title of strongest mammal, pound for pound. Solitary except in mating season, the badger's a traveler, easily covering 70 miles in search of a vacant territory. Since it must eat the equivalent of a prairie dog a day, summer and winter, it cannot hibernate.

BEARS

Who's afraid of the big bad bear? Almost everyone, and for good reasons. The clawed paw of an adult bear can strike like a hurricane. The two species of bears found in the Pacific Northwest—black (*Ursus americanus*) and grizzly (*U. arctos horribilis*)—are the Northwest's only large predators that eat both meat and plants.

Although meat-eaters when salmon, rodents, carrion, and fawns of elk and deer are plentiful, they are content with nuts, berries, bulbs, grasses, and aquatic vegetation. The grizzly has a phenomenal memory for the plants in its territory: where they are and when each matures. The black bear claws off the outer bark of trees to get at the sweet, high-energy sapwood under it, badly damaging trees, especially young Douglas firs and hemlocks. A single bear can peel 50 to 60 young trees a day, killing many of them.

The Northwest has the largest black bear population in the Lower 48, and it is increasing. Of the estimated 500,000 black bears in the United States, 50,000 roam Northwest foothills. Washington alone may have 25,000 of them. Black bears—which can be blue-black, cinnamon, grizzled, or chocolate in color—are absent from the open plains of north-central and southeastern Oregon, eastern Washington, and southern Idaho.

The grizzly, now considered the same species as the brown bear, is rare in the Pacific Northwest. Only 450 to 700 grizzlies may be wandering in six isolated western areas, including Washington, Idaho, Montana, and Wyoming, with perhaps 10 to 20 in Washington's North Cascades. Some grizzlies are believed to live in the Northern Rockies and the Selkirk–Bitterroot Wilderness of Idaho. Despite

> **The Northwest has the largest black bear population in the Lower 48, and it is increasing.**
> ●

variations in color, the big bear is recognizable by the large hump of muscle and fat that covers its shoulder and by its dished face. Much larger than the black bear (200 to 300 pounds), the grizzly, largest omnivore in the Lower 48, can weigh 1,000 pounds.

Both bears are agile and fast, charging at 30 or 35 miles an hour. Both species send their cubs up trees in case of danger. The adult black bear can follow them up, but the grizzly soon becomes too heavy to climb. It is more dangerous not only because of its strength but because of its

• DIETS TO DIE FOR •

Nature punishes picky eaters. Few predator-prey populations are so closely connected as those of the Canada lynx (*Lynx canadensis*) and snowshoe hare (*Lepus americanus*). Although the lynx can kill other small mammals, it has evolved into a predator largely dependent upon a single prey species, the snowshoe hare. In this feast-or-famine lifestyle, when hares are plentiful, so are lynx, with both species producing large litters and the lynx eating primarily snowshoe hare.

Every 10 years or so, however, hare populations peak. More and more hares browse on winter food of tips, shoots, and roots of young trees and bushes. Increasing snow depth allows the hares to browse at ➤

unpredictability. Both species will kill and eat humans, but black bears would rather flee than fight.

Both blacks and grizzlies undergo a partial hibernation in a cavelike hole during winter. From October to April, the bears do not drink, eat, or pass waste. A female, whose cubs are usually born in late January, nurses the cubs for 6 weeks, keeping them warm with her body heat.

CANADA LYNX

Huge, furry snowshoe paws make the Canada lynx (*Lynx canadensi*) the most efficient

---

• DIETS TO DIE FOR *cont.* •

ever-higher levels, retarding new growth. Less winter food is available, and litters of the hares become smaller. That means less food and smaller litters for the lynx; many of its young starve. But fewer lynx means fewer hares killed. In a few years trees and hares recover. The cycle begins anew.

Cougars (*Felis concolor*) and deer are similarly, although less consistently, linked. Cougar population fluctuates with the supply of deer.

Another complex relationship involves northern flying squirrels (*Glaucomys sabrinus*) and red-backed voles (*Clethrionomys californicus*), which dig and eat truffles, spreading the spores of the underground fungus in their droppings. Although neither animal travels far, the spores do, aided by the northern spotted owl (*Strix occidentalis caurina*), which preys on the small animals, and by the great horned owl, which preys on the spotted owl. The sturdy truffle spores can end up many miles away. (See Northern Spotted Owl; Cougar; Lynx, Mushrooms)

Canadian Lynx and Snowshoe Hare

predator on snow in North America. This solitary, nocturnal relative of the bobcat used to roam much of the North, but is so scarce now that it has been declared endangered. Notably difficult to census, the cats are estimated to total 100 to 200 in Washington, 30 of which are breeders. Idaho may have 50 lynx. It hides out in northeastern Washington's high, remote old-growth lodgepole pine forests in the Pasayten Wilderness of the Okanogan National Forest, roaming several hundred thousand acres above 5,000 feet elevation, where snow can remain until August.

The tawny lynx sports distinctive black, pointed tufts of hair at the ear tips, a stubby bobtail tipped in black, and a ruff of hair around the face. Just 2 feet high at the shoulder and weighing less than 30 pounds, the lynx looks larger with its dense fur, huge feet, and fairly long legs, all of which help it move in deep snow. In winter heavy pads of fur grow on its outsized paws, insulating and supporting them in soft snow.

The lynx is more curious than aggressive. Despite horrible screams during breeding and male arguments, the animals evidently don't fight, to judge from virtually scar-free pelts.

When pursuing snowshoe hares, its primary food source, the seldom-glimpsed cat can leap up to 20 feet and run 20 to 25 miles an hour in short bursts, ideal for its freeze-and-dash method of hunting. Only flood, fire, and starvation drive the lynx from its territory. Hunger sends the animal to open tundra and plains, where it kills snowbound deer, small mammals, and even porcupines. (See Diets to Die For)

COUGAR

Graceful, curious, stealthy, independent, powerful. The cougar (*Felis concolor*), also known as puma, panther, and mountain lion, once enjoyed one of the widest distributions of any single species of mammal in the western hemisphere. It lived in deserts, swamps, forests, and mountains in all the contiguous states. Now, elevated from predator to game animal, only an estimated 5,000 cougars survive, primarily in western wilderness. All three Northwest states provide ideal cougar country—rugged mountain terrain with sparsely wooded canyons inhabited by large game, deer preferred.

The cougar, largest of three native Northwest cats, is the last big carnivore that resides in significant numbers in the Lower 48. A large male, weighing 200 pounds, can measure 9 feet, including a tail one-third its body length. It survives in the Northwest largely because so much public land has been set aside in wilderness and national forests and parks.

Using stealth and ambush, the cougar, the nation's most skillful large carnivore, makes a quick, clean kill 80 percent of the time. Unlike other solitary predators, it often attacks a prey larger than itself, such as an elk weighing 800 pounds. By defending its territory from other cougars, the animal protects its own deer herds. Recent sightings of cougars may have been caused by human encroachment into cougar territory, or by nearly grown cougars seeking to establish a territory.

Although a stalking cougar is moon silent, it can produce prolonged, spine-tingling screams during mating or in defense of territory. It also purrs, snarls, coos, whistles, mews, yowls, and growls. The tawny-coated cougar

> **Using stealth and ambush, the cougar makes a quick, clean kill 80 percent of the time.**

leaves distinctive pawprints 7 inches wide, combined with an extra-long stride. (See Diets to Die For)

MARMOTS

"Seize the summer"—a marmot's motto. It spends 8 or 9 months of each year underground in the most complete hibernation of any animal. These largest members of the squirrel family, up to 30 inches long, can weigh 16 to 20 pounds before putting on hibernation fat. With so few months above ground, marmots bask in the sun, feast and frolic, and gather wildflowers (a favorite food) while they may. The playful yearlings box, wrestle, and chew on each other. The marmot colony, which may total a dozen members, is sociable: Each morning they greet each other, touching mouths, nibbling necks and ears, rubbing noses and cheeks (where scent glands abound).

The hoary marmot (*Marmota caligata*) is the largest North American marmot, with black feet, a black and silver head, and silvery gray fur on its back— camouflage against the gray granite above timberline. Smaller yellow-bellied marmots (*M. flaviventris*) live at lower elevations of the Cascades and Rockies, on rock outcroppings and talus slides. The only marmot species in Oregon, the yellow-bellied marmots are also found in eastern Washington and northern Idaho. The Olympic marmot species (*M. olympus*), which lives only in the high country of Olympic National Park, may be an offshoot of the alpine hoary marmot. The unique Olympic marmot has a grizzled brown coat and brown feet, distinctive white muzzle, and white areas near the eyes.

Marmots use permanent burrow systems covering perhaps 5 acres and extending as much as 14 feet into the hillside, with the entrance under or between boulders. Even a bear seldom can dig one out. Marmot mothers hibernate with their yearlings in a special burrow lined with grass.

Active during the day and plump with stored fat, marmots are coveted by fox,

golden eagle, coyote, cougar, and bear. They must be eternally vigilant. Any member may sound the shrill whistle that sends all marmots within hearing distance into an escape burrow. A long whistle means "predator in sight"; a descending note means "take cover!"

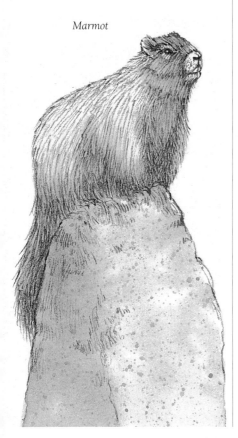

Marmot

MARTEN

A symbol of wildness and one of the most elusive of mammals, the marten (*Martes americana caurina*) is found primarily in the northeastern corner of Washington, in Oregon's Coast Mountains and at higher elevations in the Blue and Wallowa Mountains, and in northern Idaho. The marten, also called pine marten or rock marten, used to be more common, but its range has decreased. It lives in mature evergreen forests in summer, at elevations from 4,000 to 7,000 feet.

Its mustelid (weasel) family includes some small carnivores

that are efficient killers (weasel, mink) as well as the playful river and sea otters. The marten, noted for its curiosity, is attractive, with reddish brown fur and large eyes in an appealing face. Unusually noisy, it snorts, growls, squeaks, hisses, and chuckles. The marten is hard to trap in winter, when the fur—known as American sable—is prime, because it forages under the snow. The most arboreal of the weasel clan, the marten spends most of the year in trees, eating pinecone seeds, climbing with great agility in pursuit of the red squirrel and flying squirrel, and leaping 8 feet from tree to tree, using its own squirrel-like tail for balance. It will leap from tree to ground when snow or duff cushion it.

Its poorly insulated body and inability to store fat for the winter force the marten to eat constantly to maintain body temperature. So it wanders, hunting on the ground and on downed trees, peering into holes and under bushes for snakes and frogs. Like its cousin the weasel, it kills prey larger than itself with a bite to the throat. Unlike others in the weasel family, it seldom kills more than it can eat. Its insatiable appetite helps keep small rodents under control. Although largely carnivorous, it varies its diet with pinecone seeds and honey.

MOUNTAIN BEAVER

When is a beaver not a beaver? The mountain beaver (*Aplodontia rufa*), a species 60 million years old, is not a beaver and does not restrict itself to mountains. A million years ago the range of this most primitive of living rodents, the last survivor of an ancient family, extended over most of the western United States; now the 5-inch-tall animal lives only in the Pacific Northwest and northern California. Although it evolved before the families of modern rodents such as squirrels and mice, the mountain beaver has

• COMEBACK KIDS •

Good news! Some Northwest endangered animal species have significantly increased their populations over the past few decades and will soon be dropped from the list of federally protected endangered species. Of the 1,135 species listed, 29 are being considered for de-listing.

Gray whales were near extinction on the Pacific coast, where their coast-hugging annual migrations made them easy victims of whalers. But protection from hunting under the Marine Mammal Protection Act of 1972 allowed them to recover. In 1994, the gray whale was the first marine mammal to be removed from the federal endangered list. Mexico deserves credit for setting aside the whales' breeding and birthing lagoons—7.2 million acres—as the world's first whale sanctuaries. Total population is now around 22,000.

Being listed as endangered doesn't guarantee a species' recovery. The bald eagle, once killed for bounty money, was long considered "vermin." Although the 1942 Eagle Protection Act made killing the bird or selling its feathers illegal, in 1963 the birds were near extinction in the Lower 48, with only 417 nesting pairs. The primary cause was the pesticide DDT, which so weakened eggshells that the weight of an incubating bird could cause them to break. DDT seriously affected both the bald eagle and peregrine falcon, at the top of the feeding chain.

Even the 1972 ban on DDT in North American failed to increase bald eagle populations. Then in 1979 a Bald Eagle Recovery Team began to improve habitat for the eagles in seven western states, focusing on protection from disturbance during nesting. Their goal of 800 nesting sites in the region was exceeded by 400. Washington alone boasted more than 550.

The peregrine falcon was listed as endangered in 1970 when its population east of the Mississippi hit zero. The nation's last surviving 119 pairs, brought to Idaho near Boise to breed, were soon producing 250 eggs a year. By 1981, 150 young peregrines a year were being released both into the wild and into big cities, where the birds produced young on skyscraper window ledges and feeding their young on pigeons. The breeding center released more than 4,000 falcons in 28 states. In 1995 the falcons were removed from the endangered list.

The comeback road contains a few obstacles. In 1998 Washington's Makah tribe decided for cultural reasons to kill four gray whales a year for 5 years. Conservationists protested vehemently. The peregrine falcon seems out of danger, but lowered reproduction rates of some groups of bald eagles on Hood Canal and the lower Columbia River are reminders of the price of pollution. (See Bald Eagle, Peregrine Falcon, Raptor Havens, Whales) changed little during its millions of years on earth.

The shy, nocturnal animal resides in Oregon and Washington on moist, brushy Cascade slopes at elevations as high as 9,000 feet, and also in moist lowland valleys and ravines with easy-to-dig soil and a source of water. With primitive kidneys requiring a great deal of water, the mountain beaver may divert a stream into its tunnels.

One of the worst garden pests in the moist uplands of the Northwest, it is beaverlike in gnawing bark and branches from trees. In addition to fern sprouts, seedlings, skunk cabbage, and devil's club, it relishes delicacies such as rhododendrons, roses and domesticated vegetables, standing upright to nip them off or climbing to feed on trees.

Slow-moving, and thus an easy prey, the mountain beaver spends most of its time underground. Limited by poor hearing and eyesight, it seldom strays farther than 100 feet from its extensive burrows, even tunneling to food. Rather than eating in the open, the mountain beaver often drags home small shrubs—roots and all—pulling them partly inside to plug the entrance.

It burrows year-round with short, powerful legs and strongly clawed feet. An entire complex can be 5 feet deep, with special rooms for nesting, winter food storage, feces, and garbage. Mounds of dirt give it away. Farmers dislike the animals because their tunnels often undermine the soil so that it collapses.

MOUNTAIN GOAT

They climb a precipitous ridge not "because it's there" but because no one else is there. No other large North American mammal lives in such difficult terrain or can match the climbing ability or extraordinary strength and balance of the mountain goat (*Oreamnos americanus*). Predators are scarce and disadvantaged on steep alpine ridges. The mountain goat's flexible hoofs, unique among mammals with hard outer edges and a spongy-soft center to increase traction, grip like suction cups.

Most Pacific Northwest mountain goats are native to the Cascade and Selkirk Mountains of Washington, and to wilderness and national forest areas in the Rockies of northern Idaho. Although Oregon lacks native mountain goats, transplants from Washington thrive in the craggy Wallowa

Mountain Goats

Mountains, as they do in the Olympic Mountains, to the detriment of local flora.

The mountain goat's shaggy, white winter outer coat, which protects it against minus 50°F cold, consists of coarse hollow guard hairs 7 to 8 inches long, piled up over shoulders and hips and sheathing the legs. Under it is a fine, light, 3-inch-long undercoat that serves as winter insulation and light summer coat.

With four ruminant stomachs, the mountain goat eats almost anything that grows in its harsh habitat: grasses, twigs, conifer needles, dwarf willow and subalpine fir, moss, wildflowers, lichen, even coarse beargrass leaves. In winter it paws away snow to uncover food on high, south-facing slopes. With goats insisting on a privacy zone of a few feet to a few yards, herds stay small, reducing competition for food.

In mating season, males, especially young ones, feint with their short, dagger-sharp horns, stare each other down, bluff, and stamp hoofs while attacking the thick-skinned rump and belly, despite the risk of falling off cliffs. The nanny gives birth on a secluded rocky ridge, vigilant against predators: golden eagles, grizzlies, cougars. A few minutes after birth, a kid is up and nursing. By the second day, it clambers up rocks, skips, and spins in circles, with its mother guarding the downhill side. A female fighting for her kids can kill large predators with her sharp hoofs.

OTTERS

A playful mustelid? Sounds like an oxymoron. But otters, members of the same family as weasels and badgers, are known for their amiability as well as their luxurious fur. Perhaps because they have no trouble finding food and predators seldom molest them, both river and sea otters, members of the fur-bearing mustelid family, share a rollicking disposition.

Bright-eyed and tiny-eared, with bristly whiskers, the river otter (*Lutra canadensis pacifica*) is exuberant, sliding and playing keep-away with fish, but savage in defending its pups. It can kill ducks, young beavers, wildcats, even a striking venomous snake. River otters, found all through the Northwest, are at home on both land and water—freshwater ponds, rivers, and streams, as well as inland saltwater bays. With food available year-round, it need not hole up during winter. A thick layer of fat insulates its body. Like the sea otter, it takes good care of its fur, carefully drying off after swimming, especially in winter, when it shakes well and rolls in soft, dry, absorbent snow.

Torpedo-shaped, with a flattened, reptilian-looking head,

The river otter can kill ducks, young beavers, wildcats, even a striking venomous snake.

●

the river otter is a superb swimmer.

For speed, the otter churns the water into a froth with its hind legs, forearms pressed against its sides. The best swimmer of all land-based mammals bears young that are afraid of deep water. Their mother must coax, drag, or trick them, taking them on her back into deep water and submerging. They quickly learn to love the water.

The largest mustelid and the smallest sea mammal, the sea otter (*Enhydra lutris*) lacks the marine mammal's usual layer of insulating blubber. Only the dense, frequently groomed fur filled with insulating air bubbles prevents their freezing in the cold sea. Sea otters twist and turn in their very loose skin as their paws wring water from their fur and work in waterproofing oils. They blow on stomach and chest fur, churn the water with forepaws to aerate the fur, and somersault in the water to smooth the guard hairs.

Awkward on land, sea otters seldom go ashore. They wait out stormy waters by tethering themselves to strands of kelp. The sea otter is unusual among marine mammals in floating on its back most of the time. When not resting or eating, the otter backstrokes, dives, somersaults, plays tag. In a crisis—a distress scream from her pup—the mother flips onto her belly and swims, using arms and flippers. A bald eagle sometimes snatches a very young pup, but most animals won't risk the adult otter's powerful teeth and jaws.

To maintain its body temperature, a sea otter must eat about 20 pounds of food—crabs, sea urchins, bivalves—a day. The mother teaches its young to search for food, to reach into crevices, feel around the holdfasts of kelp, burrow in silt

with the head, even turn over rocks. Before surfacing, the sea otter stows its catch in an area of loose skin from midchest to underarm, and may bring up rocks to use as hammer and anvil, although its flattened molars can crush softer bivalves. (Diets to Die For; Comeback Kids)

PACIFIC HARBOR SEAL

Like a fish out of water, the shy harbor seal (*Phoca vitulina richardii*) is helpless on land. Its short arms and rear flippers, which cannot rotate forward for walking, are virtually useless. But in the water it is graceful and powerful, able to dive nearly 300 feet deep and remain underwater 20 minutes. When pursued— some orcas relish seals—it can swim at 15 knots. Yet the Pacific harbor seal, one of the true earless seals and the Northwest's most abundant sea mammal, spends much of its time on land, where it wriggles along like an inchworm, never venturing far from salt water.

Large numbers of the appealingly big-eyed seals, 4 to 7 feet long and weighing 250 to 300 pounds, are seen throughout coastal and inland Pacific Northwest waters, especially in estuaries and at low tide. The harbor seal hauls out to rest and digest recent catches of herring, hake, squid, octopus, and, sometimes, salmon. Sites for hauling out are usually isolated— sandbars and spits, islets, marine estuaries, and sheltered harbors. Although the seals are antisocial, good haul-out sites are rare, so groups share them. They don't defend a territory. A group of 70 or 80 live on an island off Oregon's Newport Marine Gardens. Others live in the Umpqua River estuary. In Washington they favor Grays Harbor and the lower Columbia River, Hood Canal, greater

Puget Sound, and reefs of the San Juan Islands.

It is the only seal that breeds in the coastal waters of Washington and Oregon. While still in the womb, harbor seal pups complete a molt of pure white hair, a color useful only on Arctic ice. Far more practical in southern waters is the adult bluish-gray hair camouflaged with dark and light spots and rings. Pups are born on isolated sites at low tide, far from predators. Harbor seal pups are unusual in being able to swim soon after birth, by the time the tide comes back. (See Whale)

> **The pronghorn antelope can cruise at 35 miles an hour and reach 70 miles an hour in short bursts.**
>
> ●

PRONGHORN ANTELOPE

The Northwest's fastest land animal can outrun the cheetah over distances of more than 1,000 yards. Aided by large heart and lungs, powerful muscles, very strong leg bones, and padded hoofs, the pronghorn antelope (*Antilocapra americana*) can cruise at 35 miles an hour and reach 70 miles an hour in short bursts. Only 3 feet high at the shoulders, the pronghorn depends on speed, hearing, and eyesight to protect itself in its open habitat from golden eagles and coyotes. The pronghorns' large, heavily lashed eyes, eight times keener than human eyes, can spot predators 3 miles away. To warn the herd of danger, each pronghorn raises 3-inch-long hairs on a white rump rosette.

The pronghorn, a North American native, is not a true antelope. It is the last living species of a prehistoric family

Pronghorn Antelope

of grazers. In the early 1800s pronghorns totaled about 40 million. Within 100 years hunters had almost exterminated them. Now, they may number several million in all the West.

Idaho's pronghorn population lives in several valleys of the arid southeastern Snake River Plain. Although eastern Washington has a few imported pronghorn, Washington lacks a prolonged spring, vast grassland ranges, and abundant summer water to sustain a herd. One of the largest Northwest herds browses in Oregon's Hart Mountain National Antelope Refuge, a high-desert mountain oasis with springs and abundant desert sagebrush, a favorite pronghorn food. In the fall the small feeding groups of summer move down from higher elevations. Even though unable to move well in deep snow, they descend no farther than necessary, pawing through snow to find food.

The handsome animal sports a coarse, orangish brown coat, two white bands on the neck, and a black strip up the snout. Muscles in the skin move hollow hairs of the coarse coat up for cooling, and down for below-zero protection. It is the only true horned animal in the world to annually shed its outer sheath of black, fused, hairlike keratin. Unlike other horns, the pronghorn's heavy, 20-inch-long horns branch, curving backward with a prong projecting forward. During mating season, young pronghorn bachelors thrust and parry harmlessly with their sharp horns. (See Big Sagebrush)

ROOSEVELT ELK

Unforgettable! The most memorable sound made by any North American animal may be the Roosevelt elk's (*Cervus elaphus roosevelti*) distinctive bugling. That unique sound, heard in rutting season when male elk hope to attract a harem by challenging or intimidating other males, begins with a low growl or moan, climbs to a clear yodel, and ends with several coughing grunts.

The Roosevelt elk ranks as the largest land mammal of the Northwest coast, second in size within the deer family to the moose. More than 5,000 elk live within Olympic National Park—the last large, unmanaged population in the Lower 48. Another 1,500 may have migrated into Olympic National Forest. These elk were once abundant on the west side of the Cascades, but now only isolated herds exist in western Oregon, northern California, and Washington.

Larger than its Rocky Mountain cousin, the Roosevelt bull measures 4^1/$_2$ to 5 feet at the shoulder, weighs 800 to 1,000 pounds, and measures up to 9 feet long. More agile than the Rocky Mountain species, the male may race through thick timber, even with antlers full-grown. Both male and female often display a black mane and pale yellowish

rump patch, striking against the reddish brown hair. A mature cow familiar with food sources, shelter, and trails leads the herd. Bulls join bachelor herds when quite young. Intolerant of human disturbance, especially on their open winter ranges, elk seek wallows, travel corridors, and foraging meadows with cover nearby.

Soon after the snow melts, they migrate to high alpine meadows and graze on succulent plants until snow forces them down to the low forest valleys. Winter foods are not nutritious—twigs, dry grass, liverworts, shrubs, mosses, and lichens—so the elk often strip bark from trees. As they nibble, they keep the floor of the rain forest open and meadowlike.

The first large mammals to return to Mount St. Helens after the 1980 eruption were Roosevelt elk. Herds browsed on newly planted tree seedlings, leaving behind hoofprints that broke up the ashy crust and helped seed germination.

(See Volcanoes Ancient and Modern)

SQUIRRELS

The northern flying squirrel (*Gaucomys sabrinus*) has made an art of sky-gliding. A thin soaring membrane covered on both sides with soft, silky hair runs along each side of the body, wrist to ankle. When on the ground or climbing, the squirrel folds the membranes. In the nest they serve as baby blanket and winter comforter.

Common throughout northwestern coniferous forests, except in arid southeastern Oregon and southwestern Idaho, the flying squirrel is nocturnal and thus seldom seen, resting for much of the day in its large summer nest of bark and twigs.

Most squirrel species are active all year, but flying squirrels retreat in cold weather to a nest in the

> **During a "flight" of 300 feet, the northern flying squirrel can swoop, twist, turn, and spiral, changing direction to avoid obstacles or predators.**
>
> ●

hollow of a rotten log or snag up to 30 feet high, huddling with as many as nine relatives and occasionally emerging to forage. Although not a true hibernator, it builds up a fat layer during summer and fall, and caches food for winter. It may forage on the forest floor for seeds, nuts, and lichens, but it scurries up a tree when alarmed. Flying squirrels in truffle country descend to dig the strong-smelling, fleshy, underground mushrooms, risking capture by owls if they linger on the ground.

To "fly," the squirrel leaps out from a tree—perhaps 100 feet high—and spreads its four limbs to stretch out the membranes. During a "flight" of 300 feet, the squirrel can swoop, twist, turn, and spiral, changing direction to avoid obstacles or predators. To cushion the shock of landing on the lower limb of another tree or a fallen log, the squirrel turns its body upward, reaching out with all four limbs and holding its tail down.

Two native Northwest squirrels are more conventional: the friendly, curious Douglas squirrel (*Tamasciurus douglasi*), called the "chickaree," and the much larger, shy western gray (*Sciurus griseus*), not to be confused with the urbanized eastern gray. The Douglas squirrel weighs only 6 to 7 ounces; the western gray, up to 1³/₄ pounds. The former has dark brown upper and side surfaces with an orangish undersurface. The latter, much less common, flaunts a silvery gray upper surface and sides, with a whitish belly. The chickaree, which scolds and chatters a great deal while noisily defending its home range or engaging in acrobatics, is common in the Cascade Mountains of Washington and Oregon, and in Oregon's Coast Range.

STELLER SEA LION

If you hear a growly, throaty roar, look for a northern or Steller sea lion (*Eumetopias jubata*). Its leonine mane and size match its roar. The largest Steller males are three times larger than their females, and twice the size of the California sea lion. Steller sea lions are much more common in Oregon's coastal waters than in Washington's, where there are few safe, isolated beaches or rocks suitable for breeding and rearing sea lion young. Oregon's Steller sea lions are holding their own in numbers.

Normally, these largest of American sea lions and largest of the eared seals breed offshore on Oregon's many isolated coastal islands and rocks. One herd of about 200 is unique in breeding on the Oregon mainland. They have taken over a natural sea cave (Sea Lion Cave), perhaps the world's largest, scoured out of a headland. Rocky ledges outside the cave are ideal for their harems of 20 or more females. For 2 months the males will not leave their territory, even to eat. They noisily defend their less-than-faithful harem members. Despite their massive forequarters and muscular neck, sea lions' full-throated roars replace violent encounters, which could be bloody between males each weighing a ton or more. Female Steller sea lions, however, often kill orphan pups.

Much of the male's weight is body fat, stored up for the breeding seaon. The thick blubber insulates against ocean cold and makes the sea lion buoyant. Searching for squid and fish, the Steller sea lion can dive 600 feet deep, swimming up to 17 miles an hour with a breaststroke, instead of using fishlike movements. The sea lion, which probably evolved from bears, swims more powerfully than a seal, using stronger, more supple, paddlelike forelimbs. Unlike the seal, the sea lion is at ease on land, where it can lope along, its flippers long enough to rotate under the body and lift it clear of the ground. (See Caves)

WHALES

It's a whale of a tale. The round trip of 12,000 miles undertaken each year by the gray whales (*Eschrichtius robustus*) ranks as one of the world's longest, largest annual migrations by mammals. In November and December nearly 22,000 gray whales swim from summer feeding grounds in Arctic seas to lagoons in Baja California to mate and give birth. They retrace their journey in spring. Gray whales, most primitive and ancient of the baleen (toothless) whales, fatten up for their trip south by scooping up more than half a ton a day of tiny crustaceans from the bottom

> **Despite their weight, orcas are among the fastest mammals in the sea.**
>
> ●

of shallow bays. While migrating, they eat very little. They swim close enough to shore to be visible to whale-watchers, maintaining a pace of 3 to 5 miles per hour.

Pregnant females, eager to reach the nursery lagoon, lead the southward-bound group, alone or in pairs. The others follow in groups as large as 30. On the return trip north, females with calves are last to leave the lagoons, often pausing to feed or rest.

The orca (*Orca orcinus*) is called "killer whale" but is the largest of the true dolphins. Orcas have swum Pacific Northwest waters for thousands of years, entering Puget Sound after the continental ice sheet melted and salt water flowed in. Three pods of orcas, totaling around 90 animals, circulate year-round in greater Puget Sound. At Lime Kiln Point State Park on San Juan Island, orca-watchers can see, and hear through hydrophones, orcas passing only 20 feet from land.

Females dominate each pod, with several generations feeding, traveling, and socializing together. The orca is rare among marine mammals in staying with its extended family for life. In the wild, a female lives 60 to 100 years; the male, 40 to 50. Each pod speaks its own dialect.

Despite their weight—6 to 7 tons for females, 10 to 11 tons for males—orcas are among the fastest mammals in the sea, capable of brief spurts at 35 miles an hour, and a single leap 30 to 45 feet long. Puget Sound's resident orcas feed on fish, but transient pods that occasionally enter the sound devour marine mammals, including 2,000-pound sea lions and whales. In the open sea, orcas attack other whales in a pack, each using its 12 pairs of sharp, interlocking teeth. Once shot as "salmon thieves" and captured for marine parks, orcas are now protected by the Marine Mammals Protection Act. (See Comeback Kids)

· R E P T I L E S ,
A M P H I B I A N S , & F I S H ·

HALIBUT

A halibut large enough to swallow fishermen in a canoe? That's what Northwest Coast Indian myths relate. Coastal tribes have been catching Pacific halibut *(Hippoglossus stenolepsis)* in the Strait of Juan de Fuca and seaward for at least 2,750 years. Native halibut fishermen paddled long fishing canoes 20 miles off the Olympic Peninsula, using fishing line made of thin stipes of giant kelp or twisted red-cedar bark. They killed the big fish with a

Pacific Halibut

hardwood club 20 inches long. The strange side-by-side halibut eyes were a popular motif on totem poles and other art. Large halibut are still caught along the northern Washington coast off Cape Flattery, in the Strait of Juan de Fuca, and in Oregon between Newport and Nestucca.

The eyes of a newly hatched halibut are normally placed, but the left eye soon begins to drift over the snout, ending up above the right eye; the flatfish then swims with its left side down. The halibut resembles other flatfish in changing color on its right, upper side to match the substrate. If the head rests on sand and the body on mud, the head will be pale and the body dark brown—perfect camouflage, controlled by the eyes. Unlike most sedentary flatfish, the halibut moves its entire body and strong tail as it actively pursues squid, octopus, cod, herring, flounder, and crabs 7 inches across. Sharp teeth stud the

powerful jaws. Mature halibut migrate seasonally from shallow water in the summer to deeper water in winter.

A member of the flounder family, the slow-growing halibut ranks among the largest species of fish in the sea, with the most elongated and plump body of any flatfish. Females are twice the length of males. Hundred-pounders are still caught; one record-size halibut taken in Washington waters weighed 240 pounds.

NORTHERN PACIFIC RATTLESNAKE

In the Pacific Northwest you are 10 times more likely to die from a bee or wasp sting than from the bite of a rattler. The northern Pacific rattlesnake (*Crotalus virides oregonus*) is one of several subspecies of the western rattlesnake, the largest snake in the Pacific Northwest and its only poisonous one. Although not aggressive, the northern Pacific rattler, like all rattlers, should be respected.

This rattler is found in many areas of the Northwest. It slithers all through eastern Washington, up to 6,000 feet, where it is the only subspecies, and in Oregon between the Cascades and Coast Range. A few live on rocky buttes in Willamette country and in southern Oregon. The rattler is common in west-central Idaho, especially in Hells Canyon and the western half of the Salmon River drainage.

Most active at night and during cool days, the rattler lives near rock formations where it can hide, in a variety of habitats, from sandy desert to woodlands. The Northwest rattler overwinters in rock dens, sometimes with other species of snakes. In spring it may be seen outside sunning itself, but at high noon it seeks shade. During spring mating, males engage in "combat dances," intertwining and pushing.

The northern Pacific rattlesnake, a pit viper, finds its warm-blooded prey by using two heat-sensitive pits, one on each side of the head between nostril and eye. It climbs trees to snatch nesting birds, and patrols the ground for such rodents as mice, ground squirrels, rabbits, and wood rats, which it swallows whole.

> **The northern Pacific rattlesnake is the largest snake in the Pacific Northwest and the only poisonous one.**

PACIFIC GIANT SALAMANDER

It's not Godzilla, but the Pacific giant salamander (*Dicamptodon ensatus*) is perhaps the largest terrestrial salamander in the world. Although the Pacific giant also lives in Oregon and in Idaho's Northern Rocky Mountains, it is most abundant and reaches maximum size— 12 inches or more in length—on the moist Olympic Peninsula. The wet western Pacific Northwest is ideal salamander country, hosting 18 species. The most imposing is the Pacific giant salamander.

The giant salamander has a rounded snout, a thick, tapering tail, a large mouth, and a heavyset brown or purplish gray body blotched with crumpled black rings. It is the only salamander to produce a variety of sounds; it yelps, rattles, growls, and snaps its jaws. The giant feeds on banana slugs, insects, shrews, tadpoles, mice, and other salamanders.

Giant females fiercely protect their young against the big males, whose bodies often bear bite marks. Provoked, these salamanders adopt a warning posture: arched back, body raised on toe tips, tail lashing. Despite its size, the Pacific giant can climb 8 feet up trees and shrubs to escape predators such as weasels and river otters.

Salamanders do not drink water. They absorb it through their skin. During the day the huge salamander hides under logs or rocks, close to cold streams. Mucus glands in the skin keep the surface moist for breathing. The mucus also makes the animal slippery and hard for predators to grasp.

Salamanders interest medical researchers because of their regenerative capability, the greatest of any vertebrate. They can regrow tails, digits, limbs, snouts, eye lenses, some internal organs, and entire embryos. Like lizards, they can detach their tails in a defensive maneuver. The self-amputated tail writhes, distracting the predator while the salamander escapes.

RUBBER BOA

This snake always keeps its head. The rubber boa (*Charina bottae*) coils as if to strike but raises its tail, which resembles its blunt head; the true head remains safely

Rubber Boa

hidden. This ploy must be successful; the tails of many rubber boas bear scars. There's more to this tale of tails: The tail vertebrae telescope into each other, forming a bony club with which the snake strikes. The versatile boa, common in all three Pacific Northwest states, has a rubbery body about 30 inches long covered with small, smooth scales; it can climb trees, swim, and burrow in forest debris or wet sand.

The boa is often found in arid regions of the Northwest, from sea level to 9,500 feet. It has been seen on Mount Rainier's mountain meadows and in many parts of Oregon, both on the coast and in partly forested areas of the Willamette Valley. It often hides in rotten logs or wet sand, or under flat rocks at the foot of talus slopes in desert canyons. Idaho hosts a Rocky Mountain subspecies of the boa.

Although related to pythons and large boas, the Northwest's only boa is shy and gentle, the region's most primitive snake. Slow-moving and harmless to humans, it is not often noticed because of its drab colors. The snake preys on small birds, lizards, mice, and shrews, killing by constriction and suffocation. It may swallow one mouse while tightening its coils around another.

Normally secretive and largely nocturnal, it may bask in spring

• SAVE OUR SALMON •

The SOS sounds ever more urgently. Wild salmon will become extinct in the new millennium unless we change the focus of endless studies that substitute words for constructive action. The issues are emotional as well as financial and biological. Wild salmon, like our spectacular volcanoes and world-champion conifers, are a precious part of our Northwest heritage.

Over the past 100 years, more than 100 local runs have become extinct, and 200 more are endangered. (Biologists subdivide each of the five Northwest salmon species into runs defined by both geography—stream name—and season.) Once, 16 million wild salmon returned each year to spawn in the 300,000-square-mile Columbia River watershed. Now only a few hundred thousand return. When Europeans first arrived in the Northwest, the major Columbia River salmon runs ranked among the world's largest, although Native Americans had harvested them for more than 9,000 years.

The major problems center around (1) harvest—three-fourths of returning chinooks are caught by Canadian and U.S. commercial fishermen before the fish reach the Columbia River; (2) habitat—loggers, industries, and farmers have all polluted waterways with silt, toxic chemicals, and pesticides that prevent spawning or kill young salmon; (3) hatcheries—meant to replace the dwindling supplies of wild salmon, hatchery fish compete for food with wild fish, can spread disease, and interbreed, weakening the genetic strengths of wild fish. The Northwest became the nation's largest producer of hatchery fish. With so many fish to catch, commercial and recreational fishermen ignored long-term consequences.

Most remedies in the past focused on engineering fixes instead of fish biology: screening irrigation intakes, retrofitting old dam turbines with new screens. Barging and trucking were successful in getting young fish around a single dam, but the frenzy of dam building presented the fish with too many obstacles.

Dams also figure in the latest suggestions to undo the damage, to breach earth-berm dams and destroy smaller, often private dams like the two on the Olympic Peninsula's Elwha River. Habitat would be vastly improved were the Columbia allowed to flow faster, and thus cooler.

Absolutely essential is an end to political squabbling over protection for the 50-mile stretch of Hanford Reach, the last free-flowing section of the Columbia River above Bonneville Dam. Here each fall 200,000 chinook salmon return to spawn, the last single native chinook run on the Columbia. Losing this regional treasure is unthinkable. (See Salmon) sunshine. During mating the male may stroke the female with rudimentary hind limbs displayed by both sexes near the anus. Snakes descended from lizards that burrowed and lost their limbs, but the boa family has retained vestiges of hind limbs.

SALMON

How do migrating salmon find their way "home" after swimming thousands of miles at sea? No one is sure—the ability may be inborn, with scent, taste, and ocean currents playing a part. Atlantic and Pacific salmon are believed to have evolved from a common ancestor that lived 2 million years ago when a passage between the two oceans was open in the north. After Arctic ice blocked that passage, distinct species evolved. There are six Northwest species of salmon. Steelhead, recently reclassified as *Oncorhynchus (O. mykiss),* have joined the classic five: chinook (*O. tshawytscha*), sockeye (*O. nerka*), coho (*O. kisutch*), chum (*O. keta*), and humpback (*O. gorbushka*).

Size and migration habits vary among species, but all salmon are born in freshwater and almost all migrate to the ocean, where they feed for varying periods before returning to natal streams as reproducing adults. The female salmon thrashes her body to make a slight pocket (the redd) in clean gravel. Eggs and the short-lived sperm are deposited at almost the same time; then the female covers the fertilized eggs with gravel. All Pacific salmon except a few steelhead die after spawning. Few of the 2,000 to 5,000 eggs a female lays emerge from the gravel as fry that will mature and return to spawn.

Chinook (king) salmon, most prized for rich flavor and fighting ability, spend nearly 7 years at sea, making one of the longest migrations of any marine fish— more than 10,000 miles around the Pacific, nearly to Russia. The largest salmon species, chinook are also called "blackmouth" for their unique black gums and mouth. A trophy male can weigh nearly 100 pounds.

The coho (silver), second smallest at 5 to 20 pounds, is noted for explosive speed and cartwheeling along the surface when hooked; even the fry are aggressive. A breeding coho male has a broad red streak on its sides and a blue-green head and back, an elongated maw, and a hooked snout. They spawn high in the river system, often in small tributary streams. Once found in central Washington, eastern Oregon, and much of Idaho, cohos are now mostly coastal.

The life cycle of chum (dog) salmon is the shortest of the Pacific species, with very little time spent in freshwater. But even though their flesh is the least desirable, when hooked they fight

> **A male chinook (king) salmon can weigh nearly 100 pounds.**
>
> ●

hard, running and leaping like silvers.

Humpback (humpies or pinks), are the smallest salmon (3 to 10 pounds), and the most numerous of Pacific salmon.

Sockeye (red) salmon (3 to 8 pounds) rarely show up south of the Columbia River. After 2 years in fresh water and 2 or 3 years in the sea, they're ready to spawn, the male colorful with red body and pale green head. When landlocked in large lakes, they are known as kokanee or silver trout, and may weigh several pounds, spawning in tributary streams. (See Save Our Salmon)

STEELHEAD

The steelhead is an aquatic acrobat, jetting from the water, hitting it with a solid thwack, somersaulting. Once considered a seagoing rainbow trout, it has recently been reclassified in the same genus as Pacific salmon: *Oncorhynchus mykiss.* The silvery fish, which resembles a rainbow trout, behaves like a salmon, going to sea as a smolt and coming back to spawn in its natal stream. A small percentage of steelhead return to salt water and come back to spawn again.

After 1 to 3 years in streams, then on to estuaries where they develop tolerance for salt water as they feed on crab, larvae, and insects, they end up in Alaska for 1 to 3 years. More time in salt water pays off in weight: 20 pounds for a trophy "three-salt" (3 years in salt water).

Each time the male steelie returns to freshwater, its deep blue and silver back darkens, its jaw elongates, and red develops on its cheeks and sides. After spawning, even before the fish reaches the sea again, its color fades and its jaw shortens.

Many steelhead collected near freshwater spawning beds show severe coronary disease with heart lesions. But by the time the fish is back in salt water, the vascular lesions seem to have healed. Researchers hope to find a cure for human degenerative heart disease from the steelhead's ability to quickly regain its health upon returning to salt water.

Until recently, the Northwest had some of the best steelhead fishing in the world. Now wild steelhead are one of the nation's most endangered fish, with 23 steelhead populations in the Lower 48 extinct and 100 more unofficially threatened. Most major northwestern coastal rivers still have steelhead runs, but they are diminished and highly variable, with occasional emergency closures.

STURGEON

The "redwood of the river"— an apt moniker for the Pacific Northwest white sturgeon (*Acipenser transmontanus*). Both tree and fish are among the largest and longest-living of their kingdom. The largest white sturgeon recorded in the Northwest—20 feet long and weighing 1,500 pounds—was caught in 1898 in Idaho's Snake River. Slow-growing, slow-reproducing, slow-moving (until hooked), the sturgeon probably lives more than 100 years. The lower Columbia River contains the world's largest and healthiest wild population of white sturgeon, one of the three largest sturgeon species and the biggest freshwater, stream-ascending fish of North American coastal waters.

Today's sturgeon has changed little from its ancestor, the armored fish, except in reduction of armor. It bears a sharklike underslung mouth and cartilage skeleton. The bottom-browsing sturgeon finds food by dragging four tactile barbels (fleshy feelers) located in front of the mouth and under the jaw. Its toothless mouth can form a tube to suck up mud

as the fish hunts for crustaceans, mollusks, and insect larvae.

Northwest sturgeon were once plentiful and little valued, but completion of the trans-continental railroad in the 1880s allowed fresh sturgeon, suddenly valuable, to be iced and sent east in railroad cars. The fish were overharvested and the catch fell from 25 million pounds in the late 1880s to 100,000 pounds in 1889.

The Columbia is the most productive catch-and-keep sturgeon river in the Northwest, with most sturgeon caught between Bonneville Dam and the Megler-Astoria bridge. In the Northwest, white sturgeon have been found in many major rivers, including the Umpqua, Rogue, and Willamette in Oregon, the Snake in Idaho, the Columbia and Skagit in Washington, as well as in Hood Canal, Puget Sound, and the San Juan Islands. Recently a tagged white sturgeon from the Columbia River was caught near

Tailed Frog

Bristol Bay in southwestern Alaska—a journey of more than 2,000 miles in 3 years. The giant fish are not now in immediate danger except from pollution in the lower Columbia. Fishing regulations on lengths and method of catching are strict.

TAILED FROG

Frog tails are almost as scarce as hen's teeth. The nation's only tailed frog (*Ascaphus truei*) lives in all three Northwest states from sea level to near timberline.

Most primitive and most specialized of any frog, the creature belongs to one of only two families of tailed frogs in the world. These tiny tailed frogs have the oldest lineage of any frogs worldwide; rocks 135 million to 190 million years old contain their fossils.

The tailed frog prefers life in swift, icy, boulder-strewn mountain streams, especially in dense forest. Highly adapted for life in these small, noisy streams, the tiny frog spends most of the day under river rocks, feeding underwater on invertebrates. Emerging at night, the frog may sit all night in one spot, feeding on insects that fly or crawl past—spiders, ants, moths.

The bulbous, boneless tail, more prominent in the male, is not a true tail but an extension of skin. The frog uses the tail for excretion and for internal fertilization, essential in the rushing water where the frogs live. The tailed female, only 2 inches long, uses her smaller tail to deposit a string of eggs under river rocks. Her eggs, 1/4 inch long, are the largest of any native frog in the nation.

The tailed frog is the only frog with ribs, which allow it to pump air in and out. Toes are partially webbed, but the long, flexible fingers are unwebbed, the better to cling to boulders in rushing water. Tadpoles bear an oral disk, a sucker mouth unique among tadpoles of the Northwest. The comblike teeth allow them to maintain position in a rushing stream and to inch along clean rocks, feeding on conifer pollen, algae, and diatoms scraped off rocks.

The tailed frog is alive and well in the North Cascades and rain forests, and on western slopes of Oregon's Cascades. Some adults and larvae even survived Mount St. Helens's 1980 eruption. (See Volcanoes Ancient and Modern)

TROUT

The Northwest's native trout should win Olympic gold. When hooked it dives, high-jumps, and sprints. Slimly beautiful, with a reddish streak brightening each side, the rainbow trout (*Oncorhynchus mykiss*) has been introduced on almost every continent but Antarctica. Noted for a large mouth, very fine scales, and a lack of spiny fins, trout are predacious, with strong teeth to seize and hold prey. Most trout in the temperate latitudes spend their entire lives in a freshwater stream or lake.

Food is scarce in cold-water, high-mountain streams, and there trout grow slowly, reaching only 1 or 2 pounds. Kamloops trout are rainbows that migrate from their birth streams into large lakes, especially in the interior Northwest, and spawn in lake tributaries. When food is plentiful, they may grow to 30 pounds or more. Like salmon, the fast-growing wild rainbow trout require gravel and clean water for spawning to keep eggs free of silt. Various species interbreed and then mate with hatchery trout and introduced species. Even within a single species, individuals vary greatly in color and habits.

The cutthroat, native in the northwestern states, spawns in small headwater streams and tributaries of coastal rivers, and is caught in alpine lakes, high mountain streams, fast-flowing white water, lowland lakes, and salt water. Some spend their life in their natal streams. Others move on to a larger body of freshwater before dawdling their way to the ocean. Sea-run cutthroat live mostly on the west side of the Cascades or in a Columbia River tributary in eastern Washington; they return to freshwater to spawn. Voracious fish-eaters when larger, cutthroat travel in schools in shallow estuary water, feeding on amphipods, isopods, shrimps, and young fishes, including pink and chum salmon. Non-migratory cutthroat can reach 20 pounds or more. (Idaho's Priest Lake yields some 40-pounders.) Lahontan cutthroat, a subspecies from Nevada, thrive in highly alkaline lakes in arid eastern

> **Non-migratory cutthroat can reach 20 pounds or more. Idaho's Priest Lake yields some 40-pounders.**

Washington, growing rapidly in nutrient-rich water.

Some species called trout are really char, including bull trout, Dolly Varden, mackinaw (a deep-lake char), and several popular introduced "trout." Char differ from trout mainly in location of teeth and color of spots: pale red or blue instead of black.

WESTERN FENCE LIZARD

The theme song of the western fence lizard (*Sceloporus occidentalis*) might be "Am I Blue!" The large, blue belly patch on each side of its grayish white stomach and, brightest of all, on the throat liven up sagebrush desert in all three Northwest states. For more color, the backs of its limbs are yellowish orange, and blotches and bars give variety to the gray-brown upper part.

This lizard climbs up onto rail fences and fence posts, surveying its domain of rocks and weathered logs. To threaten a predator, it may rear up and display its blue belly. When disturbed it runs into a crevice or burrow. When it ventures out again, the lizard may do a few push-ups and then hunt caterpillars, beetles, ants, or spiders. It can be seen lazing in the sun in the morning and hunting shade in the late afternoon.

Sagebrush desert in the Northwest is alive with lizards, but none brighter than this species. It appears throughout much of western Oregon, and flaunts its blue on both sides of the Columbia Gorge, just east of Washington's Cascades, avoiding humid areas and flat desert valleys. Active only during warm weather, the lizard may summer up to 8,000 feet. In October when the weather cools, it hides away for the winter, emerging in late February—unless a shrew has found it.

BEES

Unlike the social honeybee, several wild bee species in the Northwest lead solitary lives. The alkali bee (*Nomia melanderi*), native to western North America, and the accidentally imported alfalfa leafcutter bee (*Megachile rotundata*) are primary pollinators of Northwest alfalfa crops, which provide half the nation's $100 million alfalfa seed crop each year. Those bees, whose sting is very mild, are found mainly east of the Cascades.

These efficient alfalfa pollinators put the honeybee to shame. The honeybee often robs nectar at the side of the bloom, avoiding the trigger mechanism for pollen. The wild bees pollinate many blooms in fulfilling their requirements for nectar and pollen for brood cells. They collect the pollen that the stamens shower upon them on special leg or abdomen hairs. This pollen they carry to the next blossoms, and then back to the cells they are preparing.

Alfalfa growers encourage wild bees to nest nearby, preparing soil nesting beds with a pitchfork for the alkali bee, and bee boards for the leafcutter, which snips out leaf circles to line the holes drilled in the boards.

During their few weeks as adults, the wild bee females collect nectar and pollen in the

Several wild bee species in the Northwest lead solitary lives.

●

morning and prepare their brood cells in the afternoon and evening. In each cell the female lays an egg on a mound of nectar and pollen that will sustain the larva. The larvae are fully grown in several weeks, but they enter a resting stage for 9 months. When the alfalfa blooms again, the adults emerge, ready to work.

BUTTERFLIES

Brightening Northwest skies and gardens are nearly 200 butterfly species of five major families. Some are found nowhere else, clustered in what may be remnants of ice-age colonies. Several are endangered because their very limited habitat has disappeared.

The coastal Oregon silverspot (*Speyeria zerene hippolyta*), a reddish brown butterfly with a 2-inch wingspan, lives only in

> **Some Northwest butterfly species are found nowhere else, clustered in what may be remnants of ice-age colonies.**
>
> ●

salt-spray meadows. The adult will lay its eggs only on the leaves of the western blue violet (*Viola adunca*). But ocean erosion, human development, and encroaching forests have destroyed many coastal meadows. Several populations breed near the mouths of creeks in the Siuslaw National Forest and at Cascade Head, where The Nature Conservancy manages an Oregon silverspot breeding area.

Washington boasts one of the nation's first successful butterfly preserves, established by the Conservancy in 1966 on 14-acre Moxee Bog Reserve near Yakima. The sanctuary protects a dozen species, including the endangered silver-bordered fritillary (*Boloria selene*), which congregates in a few scattered colonies, including some in central Oregon and Idaho's Northern Rockies.

Although their larvae can survive on ordinary wood violets, the adults will lay eggs only on the leaves of the northern bog violet (*Viola nephrophylla*).

CRABS

"Keep it simple" is not an option for the crab. The crab possesses a fairly complex nervous system and specialized organs. A crab can quickly break off a leg if seized by a predator, by sharply contracting its muscles at a fracture zone where the leg joins the body. After a few molts, the limb regenerates. Compound eyes at the end of movable stalks provide mosaic vision through 2,500 lenses. The crab's complex mouth includes three sets of plates that move from side to side. Basically scavengers, crabs prey on small clams, fish, eggs, snails, and other crabs.

All those empty, intact Dungeness crab (*Cancer magister*) shells that lie scattered on the beach are not evidence of mass suicide. To accommodate growth, a crab sheds its too-tight external skeleton and secretes a larger one. The Dungeness crab molts twice a year during its first 2 years, and then once a year until age 6. During very low tides, the deep-water bottom-dweller comes into shallow water to shed its segmented, bluish brown shell. Highly vulnerable until its new shell hardens, the crab hides for 2 days without eating.

Decorator crabs, only 1 or 2 inches across, form the second-largest family of crabs. They camouflage themselves by gluing onto their carapace bits of shell, sponge, seaweed, and hydroids. Often the living organisms attached to the shells continue to grow.

The kelp crab (*Pugettia gracilis*), common on Northwest beaches or in shallow waters, impales bits of seaweed and other organisms on the sharp spines of its carapace. One species of decorator crabs, *Oregonia graciles,* presses the plant or animal material against its rough shell until it takes hold. When a decorator crab changes shells, it removes organisms such as sea anemones and reattaches them to its new shell.

The most visible and active crab on Northwest beaches and tide pools is the hermit crab. This distant cousin of true crabs lacks a protective shell for its soft abdomen and must find an empty snail shell of the right size, which it carries around. When it increases in size, it must find a new home. These crabs fight over available shells. Vulnerable while changing shells, the soft-bodied crab wriggles quickly out of the old shell and backs into the new one. (See Time and Tide Pools)

DRAGONFLY

In a state noted for airplane manufacturing, what better choice for the official Washington state insect than that incomparable flyer, the dragonfly? The common green darner (*Anax junius dreary*) is large and bright, with a wingspan of 4 to 6 inches; it is only one of 71 dragonfly

Dragonfly

species in Washington. The Pacific Northwest provides ideal dragonfly habitat, with its many bodies of water for feeding, courting, and breeding.

The brilliantly colored dragonfly ranks among the fastest winged insects (30 to 35 miles an hour) and most maneuverable, thus not predator-prone. Airplane designers study dragonfly flight to learn how an insect with wings restricted to up-and-down movement, and no coupling device joining front and back wings, can hover, take off, pivot in midair, and fly both forward and backward. Yet it cannot fold its wings at rest, but must keep them extended on either side.

As it patrols, the dragonfly watches for intruders and for a mate, with the most intricate compound eyes of any insect: 30,000 individual lenses stud each eye. It catches insects in a pursuit called "hawking," using a basket formed by its hairy legs. Strong, toothed jaws crunch 300 or more mosquitoes every day, along with mosquito larvae.

Dragonflies mate in the air, in tandem. The male wards off other males as the female lays her eggs, in the water or on aquatic plants. The dragonfly spends most of its brief life as an underwater nymph, voracious and ugly with a unique enlarged lower lip, folded at rest, set with hooks on the end. The lip shoots out to hook tadpoles and small fish, and retracts to bring food to the mouth. During the final molt, at night or dawn, the nymph climbs out onto aquatic vegetation, splits and crawls out of its shell, pumps up its body and wings with air, and waits for its wings to dry— the only time it is vulnerable to predators. Airborne, it will live only a few weeks.

GEODUCK

Forget about exercise extending your life. The geoduck (*Panopea abrupta*) burrows only as a youngster, 1 foot a year until it

• LILLIPUTIAN LOGGERS •

Insects can fell trees as effectively as loggers. Some insects are useful: They pollinate, prey on harmful insects, feed on blowdowns and forest detritus. But many cause serious damage by attacking living trees, often valuable timber trees such as Douglas fir and ponderosa pine.

One of the worst pests is the bark beetle, genus *Dendroctonus*. Since this "secondary invader" attacks the subsurface, sprays can't reach it. Often an invasion begins with beetles feeding and breeding in blowdowns, and then invading a living tree. In early spring the female beetle cuts holes for her eggs by channeling into the bark of dying or dead trees. The larvae dig even deeper. The female gives off pheromones that announce the tree is vulnerable, and other beetles settle in, boring between bark and wood, staying for years. A healthy Douglas fir can kill beetles by emitting bursts of resin under great pressure from resin blisters on its smooth inner bark. But if it is stressed by drought or heart or root rot, the beetles can eventually kill it.

The western larch sheds all its needles in the fall. That prevents most insect damage except by the tiny larch casebearer. The larva of a small, silver-gray moth *(Coleophora laricella)* has in the past been uncontrollable, eating its way into the new, soft needles of spring and carrying the hollowed-out needles around on its body like a house. Although the larch grows another crop of needles the same year to replace those destroyed by the casebearer, tree growth suffers from repeated defoliation. Recently, however, a biological control was discovered. A special wasp species is released to lay its eggs on the larvae, killing it.

reaches its maximum depth—3 to 4 feet. The adult geoduck stays put in its burrow for life and yet lives more than 140 years. (It stops growing after 20 years.)

Greater Puget Sound bays and estuaries are the home of the densest population of geoducks in the Lower 48, especially in subtidal zones. An estimated 130 million of the ungainly animals live there, preferring a strong current to carry food and oxygen, a sandy bottom, and water depth of 30 to 60 feet. No larger single mass of marine animal exists in Puget Sound. Where substrate permits, the beds are almost continuous, with three clams per square foot. Divers have found them even in water 360 feet deep. Each female discharges 50 million eggs a year—for 100 years. And yet overharvesting has greatly decreased their population.

The siphons of this Goliath clam, usually extended 6 inches above the ocean floor, are among the largest of any marine animal; one siphon sucks in food and water for oxygen, the other discharges waste and releases eggs or sperm. When a predator appears, the clam quickly retracts its vulnerable siphons and expels a forceful jet of water, up to 18 inches high and an inch in diameter, rapidly shrinking the neck.

Like the razor clam, the young geoduck digs with an expandable, expendable foot, but much more

slowly. The fleshy geoduck is most vulnerable when young and not fully buried. Sea otters dislodge and devour even large geoducks. Bottom-dwelling fish nibble the siphon tips, crabs dig up the young geoducks, and sea stars fasten onto the shells of juveniles and pull them from their shallow burrows. (See Native Harvest)

ICE WORM

Yes, Virginia, there really is an ice worm (*Mesenchytraeus solifuga*). Its habitat is limited to certain coastal glaciers and permanent snow from Alaska to Mount Rainier. In the Northwest 15 glaciers maintain the year-round internal temperature required by the black or brown worms, $2/5$ to $1^1/5$ inches long.

These true segmented worms live in glaciers, but they cannot move through solid ice. They probably slither, lubricated by a film of water, along irregular crevices caused by melting at the boundaries of the large crystals. Their optimum temperature, 32°F, is several degrees below most animals' biological zero—when body functions cease. The warmth of a human hand disintegrates an ice worm.

Largely nocturnal (except on Mount Rainier), the tiny worms descend into the ice or its snow cover during the day and on moonlit nights. Ice worms winter deep within snow-insulated ice, avoiding subzero weather on the surface. On cloudy nights they feed at the surface in meltwater furrows in groups as large as 500 per square yard, eating snow fleas (springtails), pollen grains, fern spores, and algae (often the red species that causes "red snow"). Ravens and rosy finches often feed on the worms.

NUDIBRANCHS

B utterflies of the sea," these brilliantly colored and elegantly formed nudibranchs brighten Northwest waters. Often-

bizarre outgrowths on their back and sides, called ceratae— branched, frilled, plumed, ruffled—act as respiratory organs and contain lobes of the digestive gland. The often-translucent body and ceratae glow topaz yellow, pale sapphire blue, ruby red, amethyst violet. Yet they are so primitive that they lack even eye spots.

Plentiful along the Oregon coast, nudibranchs (often called sea slugs) are also common in greater Puget Sound, where nearly 50 species live, most of them small and delicate with elongated bodies that flatten into a broad foot. Some swim; some crawl on seaweed and submerged rocks; most suspend themselves in the water by secreted mucus threads. Smaller ones often inhabit tide pools and eelgrass. Some nudibranchs live on specific hosts and camouflage themselves to match.

The opalescent nudibranch (*Hermissenda crassicornis*), only

Opalescent Nudibranch

1 to 2 inches long with brilliant orange ceratae and pale blue lines on its body, is a common Northwest nudibranch. Two of the world's largest nudibranchs inhabit Northwest marine waters. One of them, the broad, foot-long "orange peel" nudibranch (*Tochuina tetraquestra*) displays short white gills fringing an oblong, orange-colored body covered with knobby growths. A striking rainbow nudibranch (*Dendronotus iris*), with two rows of pointed gills tipped with white or purple, measures almost a foot long and 3 inches wide.

Usually aggressive, male and female suspend hostilities while mating, biting, and mouthing each other. Larger ones may even eat a smaller partner. Although nudibranchs, like slugs, are hermaphrodites, they

• TIME AND TIDE POOLS •

Northwest beaches provide a wide variety of homes for hundreds of saltwater species, each with special requirements. The tide-pool environment is especially rich in the Pacific Northwest. Almost any Oregon coast cape or headland has pools at its base: Capes Perpetua, Meares, Blanco, and Foulweather, even Haystack Rock. In Washington, tide pools abound, especially in the north on the Olympic National Park seacoast, the Strait of Juan de Fuca, the San Juan Islands, and Puget Sound.

Each low tide reveals the density of tide-pool communities. Almost every square inch of rock is covered. The pools are a refuge during tidal exposure of the beach, retaining water for its inhabitants, while others temporarily endure a waterless beach. On minus tides, areas seldom exposed suddenly reveal their inhabitants, although not for long.

The highly adaptable, shell-protected barnacle resides in almost every tide pool. Barnacles can tolerate the changes in salinity and temperature that plague tide-pool residents. Rain dilutes the salt water in exposed pools; sunshine evaporates and intensifies salinity. Closed ➤

usually cross-fertilize each other's eggs. Their egg masses—formed into soft, gelatinous strings and loops—vary from a simple coil to a spectacular ribbon.

Although most nudibranch species feed on seaweeds, some are

• TIME AND TIDE POOLS *cont.* •

up inside its shell house with top plates secured and water inside to prevent drying out, the barnacle can wait out time and tide. Evening and early morning low tides are easier to cope with.

Sea anemones, crabs of various species, including the hermits (often seen fighting with other hermits over empty snail shells to move into), sea stars, limpets, and sea urchins are among the more obvious inhabitants. All sense when the tide is changing and make adjustments. Bivalves and other shelled sea creatures close up tight for low tides, as does the flowerlike sea anemone, which brings inside its stumpy body the stinging, feeding tentacles. Mussels are well secured by their "guy wire" byssal threads.

Mobile creatures such as crabs hide in crevices and in seaweed. Those that can cling—chitons, limpets, snails—secure themselves against the welcome but powerful surge of returning water, which is cold, salty, and rich in plankton and oxygen. Predators may wash in, such as the voracious sea star, but predation keeps the mussel and barnacle population under control, just as algae grazers control seaweed. High tide ends predation by seagulls.

The crowded tide-pool community is successful in facing the challenges of its environment. Observing the creatures at low tides without disturbing them is one of the quieter joys of life in the Pacific Northwest.

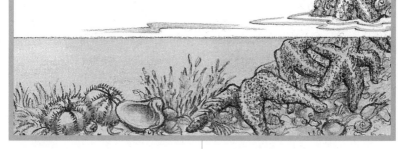

carnivores that eat hydroids, sea pens, sponges, and even tiny nudibranchs. Seemingly defenseless, nudibranchs display bright colors that warn of their foul taste. The fruity odor of some is almost nauseating. Predators avoid them or spit them out quickly.

OCTOPUS

The world's largest octopus (*Octopus dofleini*) flourishes in Pacific Northwest marine waters, particularly in Puget Sound, where it feasts on abundant crabs and shellfish. The largest officially recorded Northwest octopus weighed 117 pounds with a tentacle spread of 28 feet— achieved in its brief life of 3 to 5 years. The average Puget Sound giant male weighs 50 pounds, with a body about 4 feet long and tentacles 8 feet long. Unhampered by a skeleton, the giant can squeeze through a mesh of 2 by 4 inches, distorting its huge, pliable eyes to fit.

The octopus is the most active of the mollusks. (Its arms or tentacles are divisions of the mollusk foot.) The baglike mantle behind the eyes contains its internal organs, aids locomotion, and extracts oxygen from water. Normally the animal discharges water slowly through the siphon alongside the head, but when alarmed, it almost instantly jet-propels 20 feet forward or backward. Its only defense is hiding or flight, often behind a screen of inky fluid. It hides from formidable predators such as whales, dolphins, sea lions, and the sharp-toothed eel, slim enough to probe the octopus's hiding places.

The nocturnal octopus finds food by feeling around rocks and into crannies, using an arm to grasp a prey deep in the sand. Able to live outside water for half an hour, the octopus may crawl onto a beach or over rocks in search of crabs.

The octopus ranks as the most intelligent invertebrate, equipped with the most complex, highly developed brain and eyes and the most sophisticated nervous system of any mollusk. Although antisocial among its own kind, an aquarium octopus enjoys people.

The shy octopus becomes bold when mating. The two animals writhe around for hours, while waves of color, indicating emotion, wash over their bodies. Soon after transferring a sac of sperm into the female's intake gills, the male octopus dies. The female attaches strings of some 50,000 eggs to the ceiling of a rocky cave with a tiny opening. Constantly cleaning the eggs with tentacle tips, aerating and spraying them, she doesn't eat. She dies just before the eggs hatch.

SEA STARS

Pacific Northwest marine waters are awash with the world's largest number and diversity of sea star species—more than 70. Greater Puget Sound hosts 40 species, some beautifully colored in rose, gray, and blue. Washington's irregular coastline provides rocky outcroppings for tube feet to cling to, and a varied, abundant food supply.

The heavy-bodied purple sea star (*Pisaster ochraceus*), the Pacific Northwest's most common (especially on outer-coast rocky beaches, in tide pools, and on pilings), climbs on rising tides to feed on mussels, barnacles, limpets, chitons, and snails. In 20 years the long-lived purple sea star may grow to 16 inches across. When it attacks a bivalve, it secures a few tube feet to both shells and pulls to weaken and tire the bivalve's muscle. When the shell opens even $^1/_{10}$ millimeter, the sea star extrudes its stomach lining and forces it between the shells. Digestive juices dissolve the soft tissue, and the stomach absorbs the nutritive liquid.

The world's fastest, largest, most active sea star, the subtidal sunflower star (*Pycnopodia helianthoides*), lives only on the Pacific coast. Up to 3 feet across, the soft-bodied sunflower glows salmon pink or reddish orange with mottled gray

> **In 20 years the long-lived purple sea star may grow to 16 inches across.**

For millennia, coastal Native Americans have harvested edible sea creatures, from limpets to whales. Seafood was so important to coastal tribes that treaties protected Native rights to gather seafood.

Sea cucumbers harvested included the largest in Northwest waters, 1-foot-long *Stichopus californicus*. Its red, warty body provided five lean, edible strips of internal muscle. Natives prepared the saclike creatures for boiling by stringing a dozen on a cedar withe and tying the ends together. To remove the outer slime, they dragged the soft invertebrates over barnacle-covered rocks.

They dug various kinds of clams, including the tender, flavorful razor clam (*Siliqua patula*) and the geoduck, largest clam in North America. Geoducks were once abundant on beaches at low tide. Natives harvested clams with hardwood digging sticks, also used to pry shellfish off rocks. While clamming, they knelt on special cedar mats, and when digging at nighttime low tides, lit cedar-bark and spruce-pitch torches.

The clams they threaded by the dozens on strips of inner cedar bark, drying them on racks or roasting them on long cedar skewers. Some of the dried clams they stored for winter food, others they traded with Northwest interior tribes. They also harvested and dried the tiny Olympia oyster (*Ostrea lurida*), only 2 inches long and 2 inches wide—smallest edible oyster and one of the rarest bivalves in the world. These delicacies were highly valued.

The Native people relished the nutritious, orange flesh of the plentiful mussels, both *Mytilus edulis* and the larger coastal mussel (*M. californianus*), commonly found in large beds on the outer coast. Tolerant of a wide range of salinity, that mussel also thrives in estuaries. Coastal tribes made tools from the purplish blue mussel shells for basket making and scraping and shaving wood. The many colored, ribbed scallop shells were desired both for the food inside and for decoration of shaman rattles.

Pacific Northwest coastal tribes knew that at certain times, filter-feeding sea animals such as clams, geoducks, and mussels were dangerous to eat, and they waited out the detoxifying of the filter-feeders, which sucked in toxic algae with food-bearing water and concentrated toxins in body tissue. That "red tide" is still a hazard for those who collect filter-feeders on Pacific and Puget Sound beaches. The most serious cases involve loss of muscular control, difficulty in breathing, and death from respiratory paralysis. The Indians could have been alerted to the danger when the dinoflagellate *Noctiluca scintillans*, one of two Pacific Northwest species responsible for the red tide, produced its spectacular nocturnal bioluminescent displays and red staining of water. (See Geoduck; Time and Tide Pools) and violet touches. Born with 5 rays, the sunflower adds more in pairs, up to 44. Easily torn off, the fragile rays readily regenerate. This predacious sea star can move a foot a minute on more than 15,000 tube feet. It inspires an escape response in mobile prey, evidently alerting them by scent. Any animal the sea star overtakes, it swallows whole. (See Time and Tide Pools)

SLUGS

Any wet year is a very good year for slugs. Because their permeable skin quickly dries out, slugs prefer humidity of nearly 100 percent. High rainfall, calcium-poor soil, and plentiful vegetation—all slug gotta-haves—give the Northwest one of the world's densest slug populations. Washington's Olympic Peninsula alone shelters 23 native species. Slug mucus, which can expand in volume 500 times, issues from a gland opening at the head end of the foot. It can be slippery (on a slug path) or adhesive (for climbing). Λ slug in danger exudes especially thick mucus.

The banana slug (*Ariolimax columbianus*), the most familiar native slug of the Northwest, is the nation's largest. During its

Banana Slug

6 years of life, this diurnal slug can reach 8 inches long. This denizen of coastal forests, often olive green or yellowish with black blotches and a keeled hump, dines on fungi, lichens, and native shrubs.

Limax maximus, one of the Northwest's few slugs that preys on other slugs with its sharp-toothed radula, bearing 27,000 replaceable teeth, is a ravenous garden slug with dark spots on its mantle and foot. During mating, two slugs may suspend themselves from a wall or tree branch on a string of mucus nearly 1 1/2 feet long. They dangle in space, intertwined, turning gently, extruding a white flowerlike mass that inserts the sperm as they mate.

Prophysaon is the only North American slug genus with the ability to detach one-third of its tail (in which it stores nutrients) when roughly handled or under attack. Within 5 weeks the slug can regenerate its tail end. This genus, up to 2 1/4 inches long, tolerates so little heat or drought that it must hibernate for half the year within a decaying log. A distinctive sulphur yellow margin borders its mantle and foot.

Another unusual Northwest slug genus, *Hemphillia*, is one of only three mollusk species in the world that display a startle reaction when handled. To escape predators, the tiny slug (1/2 to 3/4 inch long) may twitch and writhe, lash its tail, and even jump an inch or two. These cold-adapted slugs, usually nocturnal, have been found near glaciers on the Olympic Peninsula, on Mount Hood at 4,250 feet elevation, and in ravines of the Columbia River Gorge.

SQUID

Shades of Jules Verne! In August 1989 a jumbo Northwest squid (*Moroteuthis robusta*) washed ashore on a beach in Redondo, Washington, still alive but dying, its heaving body orangish pink. It measured 11 feet long with a 4-foot-long body. These squid, which inhabit Northwest waters about a mile deep and have measured 20 feet long, are occasionally caught by fishermen or wash ashore in Washington, perhaps having followed the sockeye salmon run.

M. robusta sports two rows of hooks at the end of its longest pair of tentacles. Those flexible tentacles, much longer and slimmer than the 8 regular arms, shoot out to seize prey and then retract, transferring the prey to the shorter, stronger arms. These arms convey it to the squid's parrotlike beak within its arms; the beak is strong enough to cut wire. Squid of every species attack animals larger than themselves, killing even when not hungry.

The smaller opalescent squid (Loligo opalescens), more abundant in Oregon than in Washington, ranges in length from 8 inches to 2 feet. On cold winter nights, large numbers of the loligo squid come close to shore in Puget Sound to spawn.

Squid and octopus have evolved the largest and most complex nervous system and brain of all the mollusks, with the brain protected within cartilage. Squid, unlike octopus, are too high-strung to test for intelligence, and difficult to confine in an aquarium.

Fastest invertebrate over a short distance, the torpedo-shaped squid moves by jet propulsion, backward as well as forward. The high-pressure blood system of the squid and octopus is unique among invertebrates. Fully enclosed, with veins, arteries, and capillaries, it provides two auxiliary hearts for the extra

> **Like the octopus, a squid expels a cloud of ink and mucus that distracts prdators while it jet-propels to safety.**

oxygen that cephalopod speed requires. Like the octopus, a squid expels a cloud of ink and mucus that distracts predators while it jet-propels to safety. Every major predator of the sea pursues it: sharks, whales, sea lions, sea otters.

Like the male octopus, the male squid dies soon after mating. Unlike the female octopus, the female squid deposits her eggs in masses on the ocean floor, protected only by a thick, gelatinous coating. Then she too dies. (See Octopus)

· T W O ·

P L A N T S

PLANTS

When you think "Pacific Northwest," rain forests may leap to your mind. Certainly those moist coastal forests with their soaring conifers, and moss and lichen cushions and draperies, typify one important Pacific Northwest ecosystem. Washington has at least 63 native tree species; Oregon tops that by 10. Idaho, with its mountainous north and central regions, shares many of those trees, but both species and individuals are fewer. Splendid as they undeniably are, however, old-growth forests make up only one part of the diverse Pacific Northwest vegetation.

Try thinking of sagebrush and greasewood, which dominate much of the eastern half of the three Northwest states. More than 3,000 species of wildflowers celebrate spring flings, even beflowering canyon walls in sagebrush-dominated land. Idaho's Craters of the Moon, with more than 200 species of wildflowers and flowering shrubs, glows with jewel tones amid the black basalt.

Then picture the rain-shadowed San Juan Islands showing off prickly pear cactus and Garry oaks, and the western end of the Columbia River Gorge rich with more than 800 species of plants, including 58 rare or endangered, and 9 growing nowhere else. Oregon's Kalmiopsis Wilderness accounts for 1,400 floral species, and Oregon's coastal sand dunes erupt with wildflowers in spring.

The Continuous Forest zone features mature hemlock and true fir, with cedar, maple, Douglas fir, and alder. With restricted light, blooming flowers are fewer; mosses and ferns dominate. The Mountain Meadow zone, with a discontinuous mix of meadow and forest, hosts heathers, tiger lily, columbine, and such shrubs as thimbleberries and salmonberries. In the Alpine Zone above the timberline, hardy alpine plants persist despite thin, rocky soil, drying winds, and severe winters. Mountaintops above 8,000 feet all over Idaho feature low-growing tundra vegetation: mosses, lichens, sedges, a few shrubs, and stunted trees.

Idaho's diverse flora comes close to typifying Northwest vegetation. Its cool, moist Panhandle, rich with lakes, forests, and mountains, shelters evergreen forests and riots of spring wildflowers. Several ancient cedar groves with massive, long-lived trees have an understory as lush as Washington's. Western Idaho, too, is moist and cool, with thick stands of western red cedar, western hemlock, western larch, white pine, Douglas fir, and ponderosa pine. Ironically, in a state whose aridity results from the rain shadow of the Cascades, Idaho's central mountain ranges create their own rain shadow. To the east, vegetation is sparser, with shrubs and bunchgrasses dominating the lower elevations. Higher up, you'll find aspen, Engelmann spruce, subalpine fir, and limber and lodgepole pine.

Both western and eastern parts of the Snake River plain are another world of semiarid shrub-steppe country, with a few species of desert shrubs and juniper, except inside deep river canyons cut by the Snake, Salmon, and other rivers. The eastern part of the plain has little surface water, despite the Snake River in the south. Many of the native perennial grasses, adapted to summer drought, have been lost to fires and overgrazing by cattle. Sagebrush, greasewood, saltbush, bitterbrush, and cheatgrass have invaded the disturbed land.

In short, a "typical" example of Pacific Northwest vegetation doesn't exist. Only by fitting together many pieces can you appreciate the diversity of vegetation that this region offers.

ALDERS

Here's a successful tree alchemist. Using a relatively rare process, nitrogen-fixing bacteria in alder root-tissue nodules convert nitrogen found in air into a form more available to other plants. Alder leaf litter also is nitrogen-rich and decomposes rapidly, improving the soil and helping conifer seedlings grow. Alder was highly valued by Native Americans, who carved the wood into dishes, spoons, platters, and canoe bailers and paddles; it burns cleanly and is ideal for smoking salmon. Red alder (*Alnus rubra*) is always in a hurry—it seeds quickly on clear-cuts and grows even faster than Douglas fir. In its early years this plant pioneer ranks as the Northwest's fastest-growing tree. Largest of the alders, it can reach 15 feet in 5 years, and 35 to 40 feet in 10. Old at 60 years,

Red Alder

red alder often dies of heart rot. It is the only commercially harvested Northwest tree more abundant now than a century ago.

Locate the path of an avalanche on a steep, north-facing mountain slope, and you'll find mountain or Sitka alder (*Alnus sinuata*), the only alder species that grows in high-elevation forest. Most coniferous evergreens cannot grow under such harsh conditions, or are stunted, but Sitka alders thrive in dense thickets with other deciduous shrubs. Their tough, flexible trunks bend under the weight of an avalanche and then spring back, stabilizing disturbed areas. Sitka alder has the pioneering instincts of red alder, appearing on gravel-laden soil soon after glaciers recede. A grove of Sitka alder can add about 50 pounds of nitrogen a year to each acre of disturbed soil.

BIGLEAF MAPLE

It's not just the leaves that are big: The massive Northwest bigleaf maple (*Acer macrophyllum*) is the largest maple species in North America. In coastal groves it achieves a dramatic spread of 50 feet and a height of 80 to 100 feet.

Hardly a forest west of the Cascades, in both Oregon and Washington, lacks bigleaf maples, which require moisture and rich soil. They flourish in Olympic Peninsula coastal rain forests, where their sturdy limbs are draped with epiphytes.

Northwestern Oregon boasts a state champion bigleaf 101 feet tall with a circumference of 419 inches. The giants flaunt leaves 8 to 12 inches across, an adaptation to shade. The 5-lobed leaves are secured on leaf stems 6 to 12 inches long, so that they stir and even spin in the wind. In autumn they blaze orangish red. The propellerlike seeds twist in the air as they fall, and seedlings proliferate in the spring, although few survive.

The maples grow best in moist river bottoms at middle altitudes.

• TREE CHAMPIONS •

Never scoff at tall tales about tall trees in Pacific Northwest forests. They're probably true. Washington, Oregon, and Idaho boast of a grand total of more than 100 "largest in the nation" champion trees, and even some "largest in the world" champions.

Height alone does not a champion make. Points are awarded (by the American Forestry Association's National Register of Big Trees) for height, crown spread, and circumference. Co-champion status is awarded to trees within 5 percent of their total point value. Finding new champions is the avocation of a dedicated group of knowledgeable tree-hunters. Like human champions, tree champions can be deposed—by disease, old age, shallow root systems, and windstorms. Or larger monarchs may be found. The Douglas fir championship has alternated between Oregon and Washington since 1945. The present champion, the Doerner fir, soars 326 feet in Coos County, Oregon. The largest Douglas fir ever recorded in Washington was the Mineral Tree, 393 feet high and more than 15 feet in diameter. Perhaps 1,000 years old, it fell in a gale in 1930.

An extreme example of the diversity within a single region is the Olympic Peninsula, with 11 national champions or co-champions (height is in feet, circumference in inches):

Alaska (yellow) cedar—120 feet/452 inches

Grand fir—251 feet/229 inches

Sitka spruce (two co-champions)—191 feet/707 inches; 206 feet/673 inches

Subalpine fir—125 feet/252 inches

Western hemlock (four co-champions):
174 feet/341 inches; 241 feet/270 inches; 202 feet/316 inches; 227 feet/291 inches

Western red cedar (two co-champions)—159 feet/761 inches; 178 feet/732 inches

(See It's the Water)

The bigleaf maple often grows in coarse soil in forest openings created by floods or small landslides. When coniferous giants topple, they open up the canopy for the light-loving maple.

East of the Cascades, where bigleaf maples can live in moister canyons, they are often found in the upper forested drainages of the Yakima and Wenatchee Rivers. In dry, open environments, they don't host the epiphytes that so distinctively beard their sturdy branches in rain forests.

The fine-grained wood is prized for furniture and finish work. Native Americans often smoked salmon with maple wood, and carved from it bowls, dishes, platters, and canoe paddles. (See It's the Water; Epiphytes; Lichens)

BLACK COTTONWOOD

Take a close look at that cotton blowing in the summer wind, and you'll see tiny, black cottonwood seeds surrounded by fluffy white hairs. The seeds are released by seed capsules—round, green, and hairy—attached like beads along draping catkins. The cottony debris can pile up several inches thick.

Black cottonwood (*Populus trichocarpa*), abundant in all three Northwest states, ranks as the Pacific Northwest's largest broadleaf tree and North America's largest poplar, with a state champion tree in Olympic National Park that is 188 feet tall. The tree's favored habitat is wet bottomland along lakeshores, riverbanks, and floodplains. The deep roots protect stream-bank soil against erosion, and keep the soil porous so that runoff sinks in.

Black cottonwood depends for nutrients upon the rich silt deposited by floods. The fast-growing tree can shoot up 7 feet a year for its first 6 or 8 years. The pointed spring leaf buds contain a sticky red resin that perfumes the air.

Oddly, this moisture lover tolerates the widest range of rainfall of any Northwest tree—more than 100 inches on the coast to 6 to 8 inches inland. In the interior deserts, it serves as an indicator species for flood-prone or water-saturated land. Idaho's largest cottonwood forest, which

Western Red Cedar

grows on a fertile floodplain of the South Fork of the Snake River, may be the most extensive in the West. (See Quaking Aspen)

CEDARS

Northwest pioneers so scorned western red cedars (*Thuja plicata*) that they cut and abandoned the huge, buttressed trees, hoping the soft, weak wood would rot. But red cedar wood is extremely rot resistant, permeated by a natural fungicide in the heartwood. They survive for centuries, even with heart rot in the lower trunk, large sections of dead wood, and spike tops. Not a true cedar, western red cedar belongs to the cypress family, but exudes cedar fragrance and displays reddish wood.

Cedars require 60 to 120 inches of rain a year. In moist, rich bottomland, the massive trees dominate undisturbed groves indefinitely, reaching 200 feet tall with a diameter of up to 15 or 20 feet. More tolerant of shade than most conifers, cedars once dominated old-growth forests along the Washington coast. Northern Idaho has several magnificent old-growth groves with trees more than 1,000 years old.

Northwest coastal tribes used western red cedar wood and bark more extensively than any other native plant, for cooking utensils, burial boxes, enormous war canoes, and many other uses. Some planks they split for their longhouses measured 40 feet long, 4 inches thick, and 3 feet wide. The straight-grained wood splits easily, and is light yet firm and almost knot free.

The longest-lived tree in the Pacific Northwest is probably the Alaska cedar, also known as yellow cedar (*Chamaecyparis nootkatensis*), which may live more than 2,000 years in moist coastal forests. It too has fungi-killing chemicals in the pungent wood. Yellow cedar is one of only a few conifers that grow almost exclusively west of the Cascades. Slow-growing all its life, it competes at high altitude by

> **The longest-lived tree in the Pacific Northwest is probably the Alaska cedar, which may live more than 2,000 years.**
>
> ●

rooting in very poor soil. A 3-foot-high mat of yellow cedar, spreading 50 feet, may be 1,000 years old.

Valued equally with western red cedar by coastal tribes, yellow cedar provided strong wood for canoe paddles, spear and harpoon shafts, and digging sticks for clams, roots, and bulbs. Natives chewed cedar to ease toothache, boiled the leaves for medicinal tea, steeped the seeds with twig ends for a fever, and scoured the body with tree limbs while bathing. (See Barking Up the Right Tree; Tree Champions; It's the Water)

DOUGLAS FIR

Think "fir" and you probably picture the majestic Douglas fir (*Pseudotsuga menziesii*). Yet it is not a true fir. Its genus name Pseudotsuga, which means "false hemlock," reflects its resemblance to that tree, but it also strongly resembles spruce, fir, and yew. One of the fastest-growing conifers west of the Cascades, Douglas fir produces leaders (main shoots) sometimes 5 feet tall each year; it can live more than 1,000 years. Although it grows on both sides of the Cascades, it reaches its largest size in the mild climate of the coastal Northwest, from sea level up to 4,000 feet. Farther east and south, it grows at elevations of up to 6,000 feet. The most abundant tree on the Olympic Peninsula, it is too shade intolerant to be common in the rain forests.

Douglas fir takes quick advantage of land disturbed by fire or drought, seeding the cleared land from survivors or adjacent trees, but its own shade prevents its seedlings from growing well. Douglas fir is noted for its deeply furrowed, corky, fire-resistant bark, more than 1 foot thick near the base.

A century ago, 300-foot-high Douglas firs were common, but most Douglas firs of that size have been logged. Few trees now top 200 feet. The nation's most important commercial tree, it is the top timber producer in North America. (See Lilliputian Loggers)

FIRS

They're big softies. Each of Washington's four native species of true fir—(sub)alpine, Pacific silver, grand, and noble— holds the national record for size in its species. But because firs cannot exude pitch over wounds, they suffer from decay, insects, and fungi. Fir wood, relatively light, weak, and rot prone, is used mainly for pulp. Most firs grow both east and west of the Cascades.

The stately grand fir (*Abies grandes*) grows only in the Northwest and is the most common of the region's true firs. It may reach 150 feet high, shooting up 3 feet in a year. Symmetrical with stiff, horizontal branches, it grows on bluffs and headlands, in deep shady woods, and in dry, open places, sea level to 1,500 feet. It is the only true fir that thrives in lowland forests west of the Cascades. Shade tolerant, it often pioneers on burned or cleared sites.

The noble fir (*A. procera*) is the world's largest true fir, soaring more than 200 feet with a trunk 3 to 6 feet in diameter. Mast straight for 100 feet, it produces excellent timber. Shade intolerant, this fir grows slowly at first—4 feet in 10 years— but eventually surpasses its neighbors. Its dense foliage and pyramidal form make it more resistant to insects, wind, and heavy snow breakage than other firs, and longer-lived: 600 to 700 years. Noble firs grow almost exclusively in subalpine Cascade forests south of Stevens Pass, Washington, and in Oregon's Siskiyous and at Crater Lake.

Alpine fir (*A. lasiocarpa*), smallest and most abundant of North America's major fir species, struggles at the upper edge of timberline. Normally 20 to 50 feet high and spire shaped, it survives high-elevation wind and cold by dwarfing to a shrub less than 2 feet high. Budworms, ice, and rot weaken or break the brittle trunk during harsh winters. This most shade-tolerant tree on drier mountains east of the Cascades and into the northern Rockies survives a broad range of moisture.

The Pacific silver fir (*A. amabilis*) is a moisture lover (60 inches a year) that grows only in the temperate climate on the west side of the Cascades and the Olympic Peninsula. Despite thin bark, shallow roots, heavy seeds, and a woolly aphid that defoliates the most vigorous trees, the attractive, domed tree with silvery undersides on its needles lives at least 400 years. In a good site, it towers 200 feet high. (See Tree Champions; It's the Water)

GARRY OAK

Can that be a gnarly oak on the rocky, exposed headland in the San Juan Islands? Its elegantly branched limbs and open, spreading silhouette give it away. Deeply lobed, leathery leaves with hairy undersides retain moisture and help the tree tolerate heat. Also known as Oregon white oak, Garry oak (*Quercus garryana*) can grow in drier areas west of the Cascades. The oak dominates the Columbia

Garry Oak

• BARKING UP THE RIGHT TREE •

Native tribes found uses for the bark of almost every Pacific Northwest tree and shrub, especially for dyes and medicines. They used the bitter cascara bark (*Rhamnus purshiana*), still in demand for making laxatives, for purgatives and tonics, and also for yellow and green dyes. Northwest coastal Natives even brought home extra food from a feast in a "doggy bag" made of folded cedar bark. They made extensive and ingenious use of both the inner and outer bark of western red cedar and yellow cedar. They easily lifted off stringy lengths of the outer fibrous bark, 40 feet long, but had to peel the inner bark in the spring when rising sap made the task easier. Native women worked on strips dried for a year—shredding, softening, and pulling apart the more flexible multiple layers. They twisted and plaited narrow strips of bark for rope of all sizes.

Shredded and softened cedar bark was used for towels, napkins, diapers, cradle lining, tourniquets, and bandages. Women made baskets, bedding, platters, mats, hats, capes, oiled rain gear, ritual clothing. Soon after they saw sailing ships, coastal Native people began to make mat sails for their canoes. (See Cedars)

River floodplain in the Willamette Valley, and also grows along the Rogue and Umpqua Rivers. On rich bottomlands, the slow-growing oak can thrive for 500 years.

Surprisingly, Washington boasts the Northwest's largest Garry oak: 93 feet high. Rare north of the Columbia River, this oak is found in the semiarid Yakima Valley and the eastern end of the Columbia Gorge, where it adopts a scrubby form. It grows mainly east of the Cascades, however, in an almost continuous belt in interior valleys and foothills.

A rare oak-ash savanna is preserved in a state park near Washington's Beacon Rock. And, in a narrow central Washington basalt canyon, Klickitat Oaks Preserve protects more than 300 acres of Garry oak, its most northern extension into interior Washington and some of the last native oak stands in the Puget Trough.

Long ago, when thousands of oaks grew in Oregon's Willamette Valley and Douglas County, Native people burned the oak savannas to leave the prairie open for ferns and camas, whose rhizomes they ate. They also depended upon the inch-long acorns for food, as did many mammals, birds, and insects. Garry oak produces hard, fine-grained, white wood of excellent quality. Harder than cedar, oak is twice as heavy, with an equally rot-resistant heartwood. (See Enlistees)

HEMLOCKS

Washington's state tree, the western hemlock (*Tsuga heterophylla*), is the Northwest's most shade-tolerant and abundant coastal conifer. Its closely set, gracefully drooping branches produce the densest shade of any conifer. Hemlocks thrive on the high rainfall and deep alluvial soils near the coast. Almost self-perpetuating, they often form pure stands, but also grow with almost every other species of western conifer. Both western and mountain hemlocks can live 1,000 years.

Easily germinated, its seedlings thrive on mineral soil, moss, leaf litter, and rotten stumps; most conifer seedlings in a forest are hemlocks. Young hemlocks develop very slowly for decades and then spurt in growth when conditions improve. In time, this primary climax tree of most coastal forests will dominate an undisturbed forest. The shallow-rooted, thin-barked hemlock is vulnerable only to wind and fire.

Fine-textured, straight-grained, and pitch-free, the wood saws without splintering. Coastal tribes used the tannin-rich bark for tanning hides, and made a reddish dye from the inner bark.

The mountain hemlock (T. mertensiana) endures the harshest conditions of any Northwest tree. This timberline tree prefers rugged high country in the uppermost forest zone, at between 3,000 and 6,000 feet. It survives the continent's deepest and wettest snow—up to 50 feet a year at Mount Rainier—as well as heavy spring runoff and abundant rainfall.

With sufficient moisture, mountain hemlock seeds sprout even on glacial moraines at timberline or on recent lava flows. Under harsh conditions, the tree can reproduce by sending down roots from lower branches. At timberline it may sprawl a scrubby 6 feet. East of the Cascades, the tree survives in a few isolated groves, including some in Idaho's Selkirk and Bitterroot Mountains. (See Tree Champions; It's the Water)

JUNIPERS

Are they tall shrubs or small trees? Junipers can be both. They grow slowly in their harsh environment—too dry for ponderosa pine, with soil too poor for even sagebrush. Western juniper (Juniperus occidentalis) may measure only 1 foot in diameter after 300 years. Rocky Mountain juniper (J. scopulorum) is very much like western juniper except for demanding 2 inches more rain per year (10 inches in all). Both species can be dwarfed, reduced to shrubs high and dry on exposed mountainsides— 6,000 feet for western juniper, 9,000 feet for its cousin. At the highest elevations the trees may resemble living snags after hundreds of years of storms and blizzards have stripped off their bark and foliage.

Only 30 to 40 feet tall, junipers can't compete with other forest trees, which grow faster and shade them out. But both species are sun lovers and have extended north into more arid land, usually east of the Cascades. The Rocky Mountain juniper grows west of the Cascades in arid, rocky sites affected by the Olympic Mountain rain shadow, both on the Olympic Peninsula and on the San Juan Islands.

Western juniper grows in extensive woodlands in northeastern Oregon on isolated pinnacles, bluffs, and mesas. Often it is the only tree species growing in an area. The tree grows on both sides of the Columbia River in arid canyons, reaching its northernmost limits near Pasco in southeastern Washington, where the state's largest grove is protected in the Juniper Dunes Wilderness.

Juniper fruit is a berrylike round cone, $1/3$ inch in diameter, bluish with a white bloom. The seeds can't germinate until they pass through the digestive tracts of animals. Humans value the cone's resinous flavor in gin. Native Americans drank a juniper-berry tea as a remedy for colds, sore throats, and respiratory troubles. The hard, fine-grained wood makes durable, knotty fence posts and pungent fires.

> **Native Americans drank a juniper-berry tea as a remedy for colds, sore throats, and respiratory troubles.**
>
> ●

LARCHES

A deciduous conifer? The Pacific Northwest is graced by one of only two genera of native conifers in North America that turn color and shed all their needles each year. In autumn the needles of the western larch (*Larix occidentalis*) and the alpine larch (*L. lyallii*) turn golden yellow before falling.

Abundant in all three Northwest states, western larch ranks as the world's largest species of larch, reaching 189 feet high and 3 to 4 feet in diameter. When very young, western larch grows faster than other trees in the Northwest interior, assuring it full sunlight. Some live for more than 1,000 years. The tall, slender tree is the only one of the world's 10 larch species not found at timberline. It grows in mountain forests only on the east side of the Cascades, east to the northern Rockies.

It produces one of the heaviest, densest woods of any Northwest conifer, with the largest proportion of straight, limbless trunk in relation to its height, of any North American tree except the sequoia. Few other softwoods are so hard,

heavy, straight, durable, and easy to split and work.

The alpine larch grows only in the rocky soil of high mountain ranges east of the Cascades, and high in Idaho's Northern Rockies and Bitterroots, in places so high that snowbanks never melt. It may sprout on bare boulders and rock piles left by recent avalanches.

Slow-growing, it never deforms into a mat. One tree 2 inches high proved to be 10 years old. At altitudes of 6,000 to 8,000 feet, the alpine larch may barely reach 3 feet high at an advanced age. (See Tree Champions; Lilliputian Loggers)

MYRTLE

Clear your sinuses and season your soup with the same aromatic leaf—from the Oregon myrtle (*Umbellularia californica*). The strong camphor smell makes these leaves unique in the Pacific Northwest. This coastal native tree of the Pacific Northwest, also called pepperwood and California laurel, grows naturally only in the

• IT'S THE WATER •

Olympic Peninsula temperate rain forests contain the largest stands of old-growth conifers south of Alaska. In these cool, moist forests where rain falls gently for 100 days a year, Sitka spruce, western hemlock, western red cedar, and other species grow much larger than anywhere else in their range. That growth is fueled by the highest amount of annual moisture in the Lower 48 (140 inches a year from rain and 30 from fog). High humidity and moderate temperatures allow the tall trees to manufacture food almost year-round.

The forests are concentrated in a 50-mile section in three glaciated, west-facing river valleys. The forest's special ecosystem supports many species of birds, amphibians, flowering plants, and one of the world's thickest mantles of epiphytes. Fallen giants become nurse logs for seedlings unable to compete for space. Rotting wood stores several times as much moisture as a living tree, releasing it gradually. After a nurse log rots away under its colonnade of growing trees, stilted roots result—a rain-forest attraction.

A unique feature of these rain forests is a herd of Roosevelt elk that nip the shrubs all winter, keeping an open understory. Fossil pollens indicate the rain forests have existed as a distinct ecosystem for at least 5,000 years. (See Roosevelt Elk; Tree Champions; Epiphytes)

Pacific Northwest, usually not more than 3 miles from the ocean. The leathery, aromatic leaves measure up to 5 inches long and less than 2 inches wide. Most parts of the tree contain the aromatic oil; even twigs are pungent. The slow-growing evergreen constantly renews its leaves, shedding the 2-year-olds as they yellow.

Tolerant of shade, it flourishes in the moist soil of Oregon's ravines and canyons west of the Cascades, thriving at up to 4,000 feet in the Coast Range. The inedible fruit, roundish and green to purple, produces a single, brown, olivelike seed about 1 inch long, which ejects explosively as the leathery covering of the hull splits. Where it's protected and growing in rich soil, the tree can reach more than 80 feet and 500 years old. In drier, open areas, on serpentine soil and exposed headlands, it may grow as a shrub, only 4 or 5 feet high.

Coastal Indians put the menthol-containing leaves directly on aching joints to relieve the pain of rheumatism and headaches. To discourage fleas and other biting insects, they scattered the pungent leaves around their lodges and burned the leaves inside for fumigation. Early settlers blended the menthol oil with lard to make a salve for rheumatism.

PACIFIC DOGWOOD

It's hard to imagine a Northwest spring without the profusely flowering dogwood tree. One waits all winter for the sight of it. The Pacific dogwood (*Cornus nuttallii*), the Northwest's most shade-tolerant flowering tree, ranks as North America's largest native dogwood. Unique among hardwoods in preferring shade, it grows among huge conifers in dense coastal forests, often with other deciduous trees. The younger trees need shade, but later the dogwood tolerates full sun or high shade. The 4 cream-white outer "petals," sometimes 5 inches or more across collectively, are really bracts— specialized petal-like leaves. The true yellow-green flowers cluster in the center. The dogwood grows mostly on the western side of the

Cascades, but Idaho has some in the upper Clearwater region.

In the fall its leaves turn plum, purple, and pink, and the creamy bracts fall. The true flowers are replaced by clusters of scarlet drupes, brilliantly colored but insipid tasting. Even in winter the bare trees are attractive, with branches whorling out symmetrically from the main trunk.

The long-living dogwood— 150 years—produces very hard, fine-grained wood that Northwest coastal tribes used for making bows, foreshafts of salmon harpoons, weavers' shuttles, and combs.

The bunchberry (*Cornus canadensis*) perfectly imitates the dogwood on a miniature scale, only 6 or 7 inches high, with blossoms centered in 6 large, vertically ribbed leaves. It thrives in rich soil as high as 3,300 feet, sending up shoots from an underground stem.

PACIFIC MADRONA

"The litterer" should be the nickname of the Pacific madrona (*Arbutus menziesii*). This

Pacific Dogwood

handsome native tree, one of the Northwest's few species of evergreen broadleafs, and its tallest, sheds its large, thick, lustrous leaves for half the year, most lavishly in midsummer. The reddish brown bark of older trees also sheds in ragged, papery strips that display new, bright red twigs and a colorfully polished underbark—first green, then red.

Before the second-year leaves fall, shortly after new leaves unfurl, they turn orange to red. The leathery leaves, up to 6 inches wide, minimize water loss and insulate against the cold. Madronas grow well at low altitudes along the coast in Washington and Oregon, where winters are mild. These relatives of the rhododendron also thrive in the Willamette Valley. Well adapted to western Washington's

> **The largest Pacific Madrona trees thrive near salt water on high bluffs, sometimes rooting in crevices and sprawling over a cliff face.**
>
> ●

dry summers, the drought-resistant Pacific madrona tolerates a wide range of rainfall, from 15 to 150 inches a year. No other broadleaf evergreen tree grows so well, and so abundantly, north of the Columbia River.

The slow-growing tree, long-lived for a hardwood, lives for 200 to 250 years, soaring more than 100 feet. Tolerant of hard-packed or even rocky soil, the largest trees thrive near salt water on high bluffs, sometimes rooting in crevices and sprawling over a cliff face.

In early summer clusters of white, heatherlike flowers shaped like miniature brandy snifters adorn the tree, followed by striking, orange-red, $1/2$-inch berries. A few bird species devour the mealy, slightly bitter fruit. Some Native people smoked madrona leaves or infused them to treat a sore throat, cold, or ulcerated stomach.

PACIFIC YEW

The Pacific Northwest "forest gold rush" is over; yew bark is no longer the primary source of the cancer-fighting drug taxol. European yew now provide needles and other raw material for taxol that is more concentrated. Yews, once considered without value, were heaped up and burned during logging.

The only common yew in the United States that grows as a tree, not a shrub, Pacific yew (*Taxus brevifolia*) grows primarily in the Pacific Northwest. Fairly scarce in the lowlands, west of the Cascades it averages one to an acre at 2,000 or 3,000 feet elevation. Major stands grow in Oregon's Willamette and Umpqua National Forests and in Idaho's Nez Perce National Forest.

Yew rates as one of the world's slowest-growing trees—2 inches a year. Yet it may live for several centuries. Washington's largest is 54 feet tall. The shade-requiring yew thrives in dense, mature forests. Away from protective conifers, it is sensitive to direct sunlight and frost.

Despite its needlelike evergreen leaves—sharp-tipped and prickly—the yew is not a true conifer. It is classified in its own family. The tree is unusual in enclosing its seed not in a cone but in a small, fleshy aril, a waxy structure open at the apex, which follows a tiny, short-lived pollen cone. The Pacific yew is rare among evergreens in growing new sprouts once it is cut. The thin, purplish bark of the fluted and twisted trunk continually sheds papery scales, revealing a rosy inner bark.

Native Americans used the durable, fine-grained wood for spoons, boxes, drum frames, clubs, digging sticks, log-splitting wedges, and canoe paddles. Settlers used the rot-resistant, oak-hard but twisted wood for fence posts, tool handles, wagon leaf springs, and furniture.

PINES

The first dominant forest conifer in the Pacific Northwest was—fossil pollen reveals—the lodgepole pine. North America's most abundant and widely distributed commercially harvested tree, lodgepole pine (*Pinus contorta var. contorta*), grows mainly east of the Cascades to the Rocky Mountains. Slow growing and highly intolerant of shade, the pine requires a century to reach 60 feet. Tolerant of poor soils, it survives drought, intense heat, freezing cold, and soggy sites. In coastal areas, where it is called shore pine, it forms dense stands along the outer sand dunes and rocky coastlines.

A heavy layer of resin seals its 2-inch-long cones against forest fires. After a fire melts the resin, the seeds fall out, and thousands of seedlings an acre get a head

start in the ash-enriched soil. Unsealed cones on the tree release seeds normally in fireless years.

Lodgepole pines form such dense stands that they are stunted. Native Americans used the trees as supporting poles for tepee lodges, longhouses, and travois. They cut the trees in spring and let them dry all summer until they were very light but still strong.

Ponderosa pine (*P. ponderosa*), also called western yellow pine, resists fire and drought better than any other Northwest tree. Able to survive on only 8 to 12 inches of rain a year, it grows almost exclusively east of the Cascades. The ponderosa's root system, deep and extensively branched, is the most efficient of all pines. A 4-year-old tree only 1 foot high may have a taproot 5 feet long. The hardy tree requires a century to mature but lives for 400 to 500 years. It ranks as the West's foremost lumber tree except on the Northwest coast, where Douglas fir reigns. Its clear, even grain makes high-quality door and window frames. Oregon has cut most of its valuable ponderosas, but in western and central Idaho, ponderosa pine is a major lumber source.

Western white pine (*P. monticola*) bears only a few pitchy cones a year, but the cones rank second in size among Northwest conifers, up to 10 inches long. In Washington the pine grows only east of the Cascades. The long trunk yields valuable wood—lightweight but strong, with very straight grain. The nation's largest stand stretches for 83 miles through the Idaho Panhandle National Forest. (See Enlistees)

Lodgepole Pine

QUAKING ASPEN

Noisy leaf," several Native tribes called the round leaf of the quaking aspen (*Populus tremuloides*). Each leaf, with a pointed tip, is attached perpendicularly to the long, flat leaf stem, which gives the leaf great freedom of lateral movement. The slightest breeze sets the 3-inch leaves aquiver—leafy wind chimes.

Several species of Northwest trees belong to the *Populus genus*, including cottonwoods and aspens. The trees are alike in their rapid growth and short life, and most bear large round or triangular leaves with long leaf stems that allow them to quiver in the wind. The poplar genus achieves its maximum growth near water in deep, moist alluvial soil. Seeds are minute and numerous, usually covered with cottony hairs that catch the wind.

They reproduce by cloning from horizontal roots only a few inches underground. The fast-growing suckers thrusting up from the rhizome are look-alikes and act-alikes from the same parent, which may live more than 200 years. Clones that die (at 100 years) are quickly replaced. Thus, quaking aspen thickets may have redefined eternity—and togetherness. Every clone in a cluster is the same size (30 to 40 feet tall), and each member leafs out, changes leaf color in autumn to a blazing yellow, and drops its leaves at the same time. Adjacent groups are on a different schedule.

Quaking aspens, an indicator species for water, often grow near a stream at the edge of a coniferous forest. Widespread east of the Cascades, they cover thousands of acres in Idaho and the northern Rockies, preferring land recently burned or logged. In Idaho, they tolerate harsh winters and poor soil in meadows and canyons. In eastern Washington they occupy poor soil on semiarid, east-facing mountain slopes as high as 3,000 feet. West of the Cascades, a few are found in exposed sites in the San Juans and Skagit and Willamette Valleys.

Despite an acrid taste, many animals are attracted by twigs and buds, and the smooth creamy bark blotched by black. The bark concentrates aspirinlike compounds used by pioneers to replace quinine and to reduce pain and inflammation.

SPRUCES

Only five tree species in the world can pump sap and nutrients 300 feet up, including Sitka spruce (*Picea sitchensis*), the largest Northwest spruce. Sitka spruce, which grows along some 2,000 miles of the northern Pacific shore, dominates the rainforest valleys of the Pacific Northwest. In them the massive spruce reaches more than 300 feet in 800 years and boasts a diameter of 8 to 10 feet.

It prefers the rainy, foggy west side of the Olympic Peninsula, seldom growing more than 30 miles inland. Benefitting from more than 140 inches of rain a year, it grows quickly—175 feet in 100 years. Sitka spruce rarely grows at elevations of above 1,500 feet anywhere. Not common in the Puget lowlands, it grows on sea stacks or rocky coastal cliffs of Oregon and Washington—a good perch for eagles.

Its wood ranks first in the world in strength-to-weight ratio. Pound for pound, it is stronger

> **Very long fibers make Sitka spruce ideal for piano sounding boards, with resonance and fidelity to pitch.**
>
> ●

than steel, easier to repair, and better able to absorb shock. Very long fibers make it ideal for piano sounding boards, with resonance and fidelity to pitch. The spruce was also used in wing bracing and spars in airplanes before aluminum was used.

The smaller Engelmann spruce (*P. engelmannii*) has the widest elevation range of any Northwest tree— sea level to 9,000 feet in the interior Northwest. Although much more common east of the Cascades, some stands thrive in the rain-shadow zone of the San Juan Islands. Slow-growing and very shade-tolerant, this spruce grows rapidly into space opened up when other trees die. At its maximum height of 213 feet, it towers over many trees; at timberline it often dwarfs and sprawls. In sheltered sites at high altitude, however, it can reach 90 feet.

Weeping spruce (*P. breweriana*), the rarest spruce, grows in the Kalmiopsis Wilderness of southwestern Oregon's Siskiyou Mountains. The most beautiful conifer, with soft needles and graceful, outward-sweeping branches, normally grows 50 to 100 feet high, but the nation's largest soars 170 feet. It grows only on serpentine soil, often near the rare Port Orford cedar. (See Tree Champions; It's the Water)

BEARGRASS

Bears do eat beargrass (*Xerophyllum tenax*), but not its rough, tough leaves. They prefer the soft, fleshy leaf bases that sprout in the spring. Beargrass, which grows in all three Pacific Northwest states, is the area's sole evergreen member of the lily family. It thrives in a wide range of altitudes, from 3,000 feet on Oregon's Mount Hood down to sea level in Washington's Olympic Mountains.

Beargrass blooms in large, dense, showy plumes a foot long, each made up of hundreds of tiny, creamy white flowers. Stalks may be more than 3 feet high. Plants bloom erratically, with good years and bad, dependent upon the previous year's weather. Since this lily loves light, few bloom in forests. After major disturbances such as fires or logging, the plants spurt in growth. Each year, young

Beargrass

offset plants spring up from the thick rhizomes, develop for several years, and finally bloom. The offshoot dies, but new ones take over the flower-producing task.

Native Americans used the long, tough, grasslike leaves of beargrass for weaving capes, hats, and baskets; bundles of the stiff leaves were used in trade and given as gifts. Contemporary basket makers prize beargrass growing near the Queets River on Washington's Olympic Peninsula coast. Those plants, perhaps isolated relics of the Ice Age, produce leaves twice the normal length. (See Ice-Age Survivors)

BIG SAGEBRUSH

Even in summertime, the livin' isn't easy for big sagebrush (*Artemisia tridentata*), which grows in much of the Pacific Northwest east of the Cascades. Rainfall is less than 10 inches a year in near-desert regions of the three states. Often big sagebrush is the main form of vegetation for thousands of acres. The Pacific Northwest marks its northern limits.

The average big sagebrush is about 4 feet tall and may live for 150 years. Two sagebrush national co-champions—"largest of their species"—soar to 17 feet in Washington and 13 feet in Oregon. Big sagebrush is easy to recognize by its pungent odor, derived from volatile oils that vaporize and settle to the surface around the plant, making the soil toxic for the seeds of other plants. Thus, the sagebrush obtains more moisture.

Its wedge-shaped leaves of a distinctive gray-green color end with three deep notches. The fibrous bark and many velvety leaves insulated by silver-gray hairs protect the erect, many-branched shrub from cold, heat, and drying winds. In late summer big sagebrush goes into a drought-rest state that saves energy, dropping some leaves but keeping enough for photosynthesis, which proceeds even in near-freezing weather.

Sagebrush is surprisingly nutritious, with protein and a great deal of fat, in addition to carbohydrates. The almost-indigestible oils make the plant unpalatable to grazing cattle, but mule deer and pronghorn antelope in Idaho and Oregon relish it, and the sage grouse depends heavily upon it.

Medicinal use of sagebrush ranges from curing headaches to healing bullet wounds, from hair rinse to relief from stomach gas. The pungent oil repels insects. Native Americans used the wood for ceremonial fires.

CAMAS

The showy plants of camas (*Camassia quamash*) often form vast flowered meadows that resemble blue lakes. On each 2-foot-long stem, 10 to 30 flowers, iridescent pale blue to deep purplish blue, cluster above daffodil-like leaves. The

fragrant, 1-inch, onionlike camas bulbs, 4 to 6 inches underground, taste like sweet potatoes. The edible bulbs played a significant role in early Northwest history.

Dried salmon and camas were the most widely traded of all foods among Northwest tribes. Native Americans fought over favored meadows sometimes a mile long. Two prominent sites were Camas Prairie and Weippe Meadows in central Idaho. In 1878 settlers and members of the Bannock tribe went to war after

Camas

• STATELY FLORA •

Idaho chose the syringa or mock orange *(Philadelphus lewisii)* as its state flower in 1931 to honor Meriwether Lewis. The snowy, 4-petaled flower centered around 30 stamens perfume the air, especially when it grows in moist, partly shaded gullies. It can reach 12 feet high along the moist coast west of the Cascades or hugging the border of a coniferous forest east of the Cascades. Quick to appear on newly logged land along with flowering red currant and salmonberry, it blooms in the spring at Idaho's Craters of the Moon. Native Americans made a soapy lather from the bruised leaves for cleaning and rubbing on sores.

Oregon grape *(Berberis aquifolium)* became Oregon's state flower in 1879. The elegant shrub, which can reach 10 feet tall, bears great quantities of honey-scented, pale yellow flowers like mini-daffodils, with shiny, hollylike leaves (no prickles). It is plentiful west of the Cascades in exposed rocky sites with full sun. The clusters of dark blue barberries, touched with a pale bloom, yield dry, sour fruit, but Native people mixed it with sweeter berries and ate it raw. From the roots they made a tea for a gargle and tonic. The fruit yielded a blue dye, and the bright yellow inner bark, a yellow dye for basket materials and porcupine quills used on ceremonial garments and rattles.

No other native flowering shrub is so spendthrift with its showy blooms as the coast (Pacific) rhododendron. It was selected as Washington's state flower in 1892. From late May to early July, the native, wild coast rhododendron blooms—pink and purple trusses set off by whorls of broad, shiny, leathery leaves 5 inches long. Acidic, humus-rich soil and moderate coastal climate make the Northwest ideal for rhododendrons. The shrub flourishes along the Oregon and Washington coasts. In evergreen forests rhododendrons become almost trees, reaching 25 feet high; in open areas they grow more compactly.

settlers' livestock ate camas bulbs on the tribe's traditional camas lands. The tribe lost the war and its rights to the land.

Digging was a communal activity in the spring, with tribes from both sides of the Cascades working together. To dig the bulbs women used long, curved animal bones or hooked, sharpened hardwood sticks of yew or yellow cedar. They had to be careful not to harvest the death camas bulb (*Zygadens elegans*), which contains a toxic alkaloid in bulb, foliage, and seed.

The fragrant camas bulbs were eaten raw or baked in rock ovens or pits covered with smoldering pinewood. They were then mashed for drying in the sun, pounded into coarse flour, or boiled into a syrup.

COLUMBINES

It's a lovely sight, the colorful hummingbird hovering at the red and yellow Northwest crimson columbine (*Aquilegia formosa*), its head inside the flared opening as it feeds on nectar. The spurred flowers of the columbine are cunningly designed for its pollinators. At the end of a slim stem 2 feet high with much-divided leaves, the nodding bloom has elongated flower spurs with a gland that secretes nectar. Pollen brushes onto the hummingbird's head, ready to be carried to another columbine. The long tongues of bumblebees and butterflies allow them to sip the nectar and to pollinate. Ants and honeybees, however, must bite a hole in the side of the spurs to get at the sweet stuff.

The delicate flowers are mostly subalpine, common in mountain meadows where they associate with paintbrush, tiger lily, and penstemon. At lower elevations they brighten up open forests and forest margins. The much rarer yellow columbine (*A. flavescens*) brings a warm glow to rock slides and talus slopes. It grows in mountain meadows at higher altitudes than the western columbine, east of the Cascades in Washington and northeast Oregon.

The name Chehalis Indians gave to columbine means "it's good on your teeth." Their children sucked the nectar from the spurs. The Quileutes chewed the leaves or scraped the roots for a pulp that they spread on sores to help them heal.

DEVIL'S CLUB

It's armed for battle: Along the thick stems of devil's club (Oplopanax horridum) rises a bristling forest of yellowish, needle-sharp spines nearly 1/2 inch long. Hated by hikers, the shrub springs up in moist forests throughout Oregon's Coast Range and Washington's Olympic Peninsula, and east to Idaho's Selkirks. Thickets of the shrub can be almost impenetrable.

Its maplelike leaf, almost a foot across, ranks as one of the Pacific Northwest's broadest and most formidable, with spines outlining the veins on both upper and under sides. Even the roots of this deciduous shrub are spined. Its runners can trip the unwary hiker, and its spines can cause painful swelling. Usually encountered near water, devil's club rises 5 to 10 feet or more as the huge leaves reach out to gather in sunshine. In late summer and early fall, the shrubs produce attractive cone-shaped clusters of bright red berries— spineless but inedible.

Yet elk nip the leaves, and so do slugs, laying down a thick path of mucus to protect against the spines. Undaunted by the spines, Northwest Coast tribes used this plant, a close relative of ginseng, to make an infusion for treating colds, rheumatism, and tuberculosis. They ground dried bark into a powder for use as perfume, baby talc, and deodorant.

EELGRASS

A biological oddity, eelgrass (Zostera nolti) is a flowering plant that returned to the sea. (A salty environment is poisonous to most plant species.) Unlike seaweeds, eelgrass has true roots,

The bountiful berries of the Pacific Northwest range from exquisitely flavorful to insipid to toxic. Northwest berries grow in sand, open woods, mountain slopes, and cut-over or burned areas. Among Native Americans, berries were essential winter foods, mashed and dried into large cakes, yielding carbohydrates from crushed seeds and vitamin C from the berries. Bark, twigs, leaves, and shoots of berry bushes provided food, medicine, and smoking materials.

Coastal Natives ate soft berries such as wild strawberries (*Fragaria chiloensis*), especially abundant on coastal Oregon's sandy beaches, as a party food or a snack. Wild cranberries (*Vaccinium oxycoccus*) from Oregon and Washington coastal peat bogs were trade items on Whidbey Island.

Domesticated blackberries are bland compared to the ambrosial dewberry—the tiny, wild Pacific blackberry (*Rubus ursinus*).

Native tribes mixed steamed or smoked salmonberries (*R. spectabilis*) with salmon bellies and fat for winter rations. The moisture-seeking shrub, sometimes 6 feet high, bears prickly lower stems and juicy berries that vary from pale yellow to orange-red. They chewed the astringent bark and leaves to kill pain, and rubbed the poltice on burns and festering wounds.

Coastal Natives eagerly sought aromatic, mealy salal berries (*Gaultheria shallon*), which thrive in shady, coastal forests with acid soil. Clusters of black berries weigh down the evergreen shrub with its shiny, leathery leaves. Native people dipped a twig thick with berries into whale oil and pulled the berry-laden twig through their mouth. They dried and mashed the easy-to-pick berries, storing them in large cakes or loaves that weighed 10 to 15 pounds.

The berries of the wild huckleberry (*V. deliciosum*) are far superior to, and much sweeter than, lowland huckleberries. Bears fattening up for winter denning gorge on the sweet berries, abundant in many western Cascade areas at moderate or higher elevations. Tribes from both the coast and the interior picked and dried huckleberries by sun or fire, mashing them into cakes stored in large leaves or bark.

stems, and leaves, and its seeds are enclosed in an ovary.

A distant kin to cereal grains, eelgrass sends out thin, flat, strap-shaped leaves from its rhizomes, which grow in either sand or mud. Delicate and narrow, the leaves can grow 6 feet long in deeper water, half that length in shallow intertidal areas. Its pollen and seeds are dispersed by water; its modest flowers, nested in the curled leaf tips, bloom underwater. The creeping rhizomes and roots of eelgrass trap sand and form mounds, stabilizing the muddy soil while enriching it with decaying material.

Two of the most extensive meadows of eelgrass on the West Coast, if not in the world, grow in Washington waters at Willapa Bay and at Padilla Bay near Bellingham, where a 6,200-acre eelgrass meadow covers 75 percent of the mudflats. Eelgrass beds also thrive on the inner shore of Washington's Dungeness Spit. The beds shelter many lower intertidal and subtidal organisms, including tiny sea urchins and anemones, which provide food for larger animals. Migrating and wintering waterfowl and shorebirds feed on the grass, its seeds, and small resident animals.

Coastal Native Americans ate the sweet, fleshy rhizomes, dried the leaves for insulation and mattress stuffing, and ground the seeds into flour. (See Estuaries)

EPIPHYTES

The perfect guests, epiphytes don't harm their hosts, as parasites do, by stealing nutrients from them. They manufacture their own food by photosynthesis, using the host tree for support only. These "air plants" usually develop aerial roots, absorbing water for photosynthesis from air well-saturated with rain, fog, and mist. They capture nutrients from the downpour of organic debris that tumbles from the upper levels of the tree canopies. Epiphytes, which often live in the canopies of such massive trees as bigleaf maples, can be found in many moist forests, along the Olympic Peninsula's Lake Crescent and in Mount Rainier's Carbon River Valley, but nowhere else are they so prolific as in rain forests.

The Hoh Rain Forest hosts nearly a dozen species of trees but more than 300 species of epiphytes—including mosses, lichens, orchids, and Spanish moss—and the greatest number

epiphytes per acre. When wet, the epiphytes on a single giant bigleaf maple weigh nearly a ton. Stand clear! A limb may be so overloaded that it breaks. When nitrogen-fixing lichens fall to the forest floor

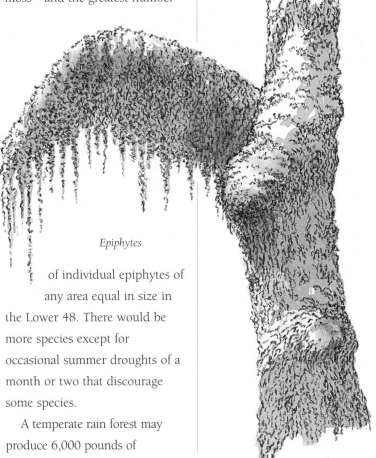

Epiphytes

of individual epiphytes of any area equal in size in the Lower 48. There would be more species except for occasional summer droughts of a month or two that discourage some species.

A temperate rain forest may produce 6,000 pounds of

• ENLISTEES •

Look sharp, and the U.S. Army might allow you to view its rare plant collections. Military bases in Washington have yielded unexpected botanical dividends, as army officials worked with The Nature Conservancy to inventory some rare ecosystems recently discovered at Fort Lewis, Fairchild Air Force Base near Spokane, the Yakima Training Center, Whidbey Island Naval Air Station, and McChord Air Force Base. Some nearly extinct, state-threatened plant species grow on those bases, including golden paintbrush, Torrey's peavine, and water howellia.

Fort Lewis, one of the army's larger installations at 86,500 acres, protects western Washington's only native ponderosa pine forest (1,700 acres) and several of the largest surviving native prairie grasslands of the Puget Sound lowlands. The base also contains 3,600 acres of scarce oak woodlands and 4,500 acres of healthy freshwater wetlands.

With public access restricted, these habitats were protected from disturbance. Some Douglas firs more than 300 years old escaped early-century logging at Fort Lewis. The Nisqually River runs through the base, a wild river corridor that supports plants, spawning salmon, and bald eagles.

and decompose, the tree roots absorb the nutrients. Trees also capture nutrients from mineral-enriched rainwater concentrated in mats of moss and lichens that grow around the tree's base.

Rain forests provide varying habitats for species that prefer to grow at different levels: on branches, on trunks near the tree base, on fallen logs, or in the crown of a tree. That jewel flash of color 100 feet above the forest floor may be a hummingbird attracted by blooms like coral bells above the leathery green leaves of Satyria, an epiphytic shrub in the blueberry family. On another branch can be found a club moss (*Selaginella oregana*), not a true moss but a lower vascular plant that grew 100 feet high in prehistoric forests. (See It's the Water)

FERNS

The very quintessence of Pacific Northwest forests, ferns are surprisingly more numerous in tropical climates than in the moist, shady parts of the Northwest. Yet the Columbia River Gorge hosts 22 different fern species. Ranked taxonomically just below flowering plants, ferns are among the oldest vascular plants in the fossil record. They lack fruits, seeds, a true stem, and flowers. But their skimpy roots, growing from a subterranean rhizome, are true roots, and their fronds are true leaves that manufacture food.

The majestic western sword fern (*Polystichum munitum*) is especially luxuriant in hemlock and cedar forests. It forms massive clumps 5 feet tall with dozens of long fronds fountaining out. Evergreen west of the Rockies, the symmetrical sword fern is represented in nearly every dense, lowland coniferous forest on the Northwest coast. Coastal tribes used sword fern fronds for mattress material and cooking chores. They peeled and roasted the starchy rhizomes and ate them with fresh or dried salmon eggs.

Deer fern (*Blechnum spican*) is unusual among ferns that grow in moist, shady, coastal coniferous forests in producing two distinctly different types of fronds. One is evergreen, sterile, deeply lobed, spreading out in a rosette. In spring and early summer, a dozen or more fertile, spore-bearing fronds rise nearly 2 feet long from the rosette.

The native evergreen, tree-draping licorice fern (*Polypodium glycyrrhiza*) decorates rain forests. It is usually up a tree, nestled in a moist cushion of moss and lichens. Its stem or rhizome tastes of licorice but is slightly acrid. The fern also grows at ground level, on bark or a fallen log, close to salt water.

INDIAN PIPE

In summer and early autumn, after other plants have bloomed, Indian pipe (*Monotropa uniflora*) thrusts up its white, nearly translucent stalk almost a foot high, often growing in a cluster of stalks. In northern Idaho forests, Indian pipe rises through the snow. Its name is derived from the resemblance of the waxy, white, nodding flower to an inverted pipe bowl. The bloom at the end of each stalk makes a U-turn to parallel the stem. This nongreen member of the heath family grows only in low-elevation, old-growth coniferous forests, in shade so dense that often not even ferns spring up near it.

Instead of leaves, its stalk is covered with overlapping white scales. Sometimes it is mistaken for a mushroom, but Indian pipe is a saprophyte with stem and blossoms bearing stamen and pistil. It thrives in deep humus. Lacking chlorophyll, Indian pipe cannot manufacture its own food.

It grows upon dead and decaying plant debris among the forest litter, aided by threadlike mycorrhizal fungi in a symbiotic relationship. The brilliant white color of Indian pipe ensures that pollinating insects will see it. As black, capsulelike seedpods mature, the blossom straightens up and slowly turns black. The pine drop and pine sap,

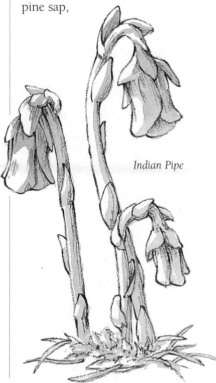

Indian Pipe

also non-green members of the Indian pipe family, form similar associations with fungi. (See The Web of Life)

LILIES

If the wildflower season consisted of only lilies, that spring fling would still be breath-catching. All lilies are perennial, with an underground rhizome or bulb. Starving members of the Lewis and Clark Expedition quickly learned to eat lily bulbs, as did early Mormon settlers who survived drought, frost, and a cricket plague, thanks to the sego lily.

The Northwest's most accessible and earliest-blooming alpine wildflowers are the white-petaled avalanche lily (*Erythronium montanum*) and the yellow-petaled glacier lily (*E. grandiflorum*). The elegant lilies 6 to 8 inches high get a head start on their short growing season in subalpine meadows by pushing up through the thinning edge of the snow aided by the warmth of plant tissues. The blooming periods of the two lilies overlap. The glacier lily has the wider elevation range, from sagebrush country east of the Cascades to alpine meadows in Idaho at up to 4,000 feet. Avalanche lilies more often grace lower meadows, even edging into forests. At subalpine heights these lilies must take advantage of only a few weeks of sunlight between snowmelt in July and new snow in early autumn. To bloom and form seeds, plants must store up energy over 5 or 6 years.

The sego lily (*Calochortus nuttalli*) is the most common flower of sagebrush country. The stem, up to 18 inches high, bears a satiny, white lily with a purple crescent inside and a green stripe in the center of each petal. The sego lily grows in open coniferous forests and mountain meadows in the Great Basin from extreme eastern Washington to Oregon and Idaho's Rocky Mountains. It also grows in rain-shadow sites in the San Juan Islands. The sweet, walnut-sized bulb survives droughts by being buried deep. Dormant in very dry weather, it sends up blooms when moisture is ample. Instead of dividing, the bulb grows larger and descends deeper, often close to bracken fern and other plants whose roots protect it.

One of the most striking mariposas is a true lily, the Columbia lily (*Lilium columbianum*), also known as the tiger lily. The fiery orange recurved blossoms are freckled with maroon dots and adorned with brownish purple anthers dangling below.

ORCHIDS

Although Pacific Northwest climate and soil are minimally suitable for orchids, 34 species grow here in woodlands and bogs. The flower structure, highly specialized for insect pollination, uses scent to lure specific insects. Most orchids are saprophytes, extracting nutrients from woody debris with the help of a mycorrhizal fungus.

The phantom orchid (*Eburophyton austiniae*) is considered the most elusive and beautiful of the Northwest's orchids. The recluse grows only in the Pacific Northwest, where it perfumes the air on the Olympic Peninsula, in the Cascades, and in west-central Idaho. This orchid flowers perhaps once in 17 years. The very rare phantom orchid always grows in dense conifer forests, undisturbed even by much sunshine. Because of a lack of chlorophyll, its stems, flowers, and sheathlike leaves (1 to 2 inches long) are usually pure white, except for a touch of golden yellow on the lower lip of the flower. Stems 8 to 20 inches long bear fragrant spikes of 5 to 20 waxy, translucent, 1/2-inch blooms.

The spotted coralroot (*Corallorhiza maculata*) and the elegant striped coralroot

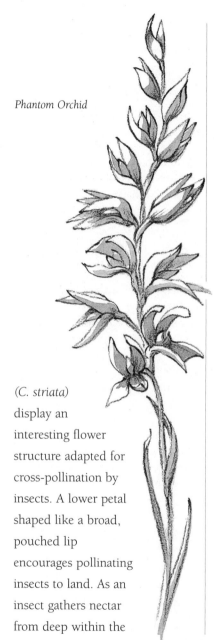

Phantom Orchid

(*C. striata*) display an interesting flower structure adapted for cross-pollination by insects. A lower petal shaped like a broad, pouched lip encourages pollinating insects to land. As an insect gathers nectar from deep within the flower, two pollen masses projecting above the lip dust the insect. Both striped and spotted coralroots send up from a coral-like rhizome smooth, pinkish stems 10 to 14 inches long, with a few fleshy scales or clasping purplish bracts instead of leaves.

These orchids can form extensive colonies, up to 1,000 plants in the moist soil of dense, coastal coniferous forests, sometimes as parasites on conifer roots. The many-flowered stalk of the spotted coralroot bears orchid-shaped flowers about 1/2 inch long, resembling the flowers of the rare phantom orchid except for color and the pouched lip. The striped coralroot, with white sepals and petals striped with purple, is the showiest of its family. (See The Web of Life)

PASQUEFLOWER

Old man of the mountain, mouse on a stick, dishmop, lion's beard, towhead babies. By

The peaks of Washington's Olympic Mountains—high-elevation islands above the glacial sea—provided an isolated environment during the last ice age. Plants trapped there by encroaching ice could not migrate south. They died or toughed it out, evolving uniquely for thousands of years into hardy perennials that now bloom in this harsh alpine world above 5,500 feet. At least 6 rare flower species are endemic to the isolated Olympic Range. Best known is Piper's bellflower (Campanula piperi). Scattered on high, rocky talus slopes and subalpine meadows, the plants, 2 to 4 inches high with clear blue flowers, root in crevices that protect them from strong winds.

Washington's Wenatchee Mountains, which run southeast to the Columbia River, host more plant species of limited habitat than any other place in the state. The peaks may have escaped ice-age glaciation, forming a high island where vegetation could survive the freeze. Lewisia tweedyi, one of the Pacific Northwest's loveliest wildflowers, protected in the Tumwater Canyon Botanical Area, grows naturally only in the Wenatchee Mountains on slopes or in rock crevices at elevations of up to 5,000 feet. Rarest and largest of the bitterroot Lewisias, each plant bears up to 5 saucer-shaped blooms 3 inches across, varying from salmon pink to pale yellow. The secret of survival: a thick, fleshy taproot extending 3 feet beyond the few inches of soil into talus slopes and rock crevices. The hardy plant survives a temperature range of minus 30°F to 100°F.

Southwestern Oregon's Klamath–Siskiyou area, where coastal fog meets arid interior air, contains one-fourth of Oregon's rare or endangered plants. The ancient Siskiyous form a complex vegetation pattern, with rainfall ranging from 20 to 100 inches. Siskiyou endemics are confined to serpentine soil with high levels of heavy metals and scarce nutrients—toxic to most plants. The Kalmiopsis Wilderness in Siskiyou National Forest is home to Kalmiopsis leachiana, one of the world's rarest shrubs. It resembles a rhododendron 1 foot high, roots in cracks and crevices on steep hillsides in the coastal rain shadow.

any name, in early August in alpine meadows you'll see the shaggy seed heads of pasqueflower (Anemone occidentalis), also called western anemone. Pasqueflower has the same, very early blooming period as the glacier lily, appearing as snow is melting. By August the

beautiful blossom is gone.
Only early viewers see the
cream-colored blossoms 2 inches
across and tinged with light blue
and lavender. Each rises on a long
stem thickly covered with soft
hairs and set off by a whorl of
finely divided leaves just below
the blossoms.

More familiar are the shaggy
white seed plumes on the end of
stalks rising 1 to 2 feet, much
longer than when the flower is in
bloom. Although the plant grows
from a perennial tuber, it also
spreads by seed. Each seed has its
own feathery tail to catch the
wind. Many "dishmops," however,
end up in the drying piles of hay
cut by the tiny, rabbitlike pika.

PRICKLY PEAR CACTUS

It's a prickly surprise, seeing
prickly pear cactus (*Opuntia
fragilis*) in the San Juan Islands.
Chalk it up to the Olympic rain
shadow, which reduces rainfall in
parts of the islands, creating arid
patches where cactus and other

east-of-the-mountains plants grow
naturally. The cactus are, of
course, far more at home in
sagebrush country.

The prickly pear protects itself
from grazing animals by clustered
spines almost 4 inches long, and
shorter, easily detached bristles
that irritate the skin. It bears a
toxic layer of calcium oxalate
crystals just under its skin.

Cacti carry on photosynthesis
in green stem joints, whose
tissue is adapted for water
storage. In the arid Pacific
Northwest home country of the
cactus, rainfall often amounts to
less than 10 inches a year. Rain
plumps up the flat joints;
drought shrivels them. Each pad
can root a new plant.

The striking yellow flower,
2 to 3 inches across, doesn't
appear every year in the San
Juans. It forms at the top of a
joint within a depression where
the spined fruit, much sought
after by animals, later appears.
Insects pollinate the prickly pear.

Nectar deep inside the flower attracts a bee; then, to ensure pollination, the petals curl inward to make a tender trap.

SKUNK CABBAGE

By any other name, the skunk cabbage (*Lysichitum americanum*) would inspire no wrinkled noses. The odor is closer to earthy bog than essence of skunk. This handsome plant flaunts the largest leaves of any Northwest native flora—sometimes more than 4 feet long and 1 foot wide, with a fleshy midrib.

One of the earliest plants to emerge in spring, and a long-lived perennial (some 70 years), this pungent relative of the calla lily and anthurium generates enough heat in its tissues to melt its way up through snow. Heat and scent attract pollinating bees, beetles, and butterflies. The leaves spring up from the base several weeks after the yellow spathe (hood) appears. That

Skunk Cabbage

134

• TURNING THE TABLES •

If a mammal can fly and some birds cannot, why shouldn't plants eat animals? The Pacific Northwest plays host to three families of carnivorous plants: pitcher plant, sundew, and bladderwort.

The cobra lily *(Darlingtonia californica)*, the Northwest's only pitcher plant, captures insects with the most complicated leaf structure of any North American pitcher plant. Highly localized, the cobra lily grows at sea level along Oregon's coast in wet, acidic peat or sphagnum bogs, and also on serpentine soil up to 8,000 feet in the Siskiyous. The cobra lily supplements its nitrogen-poor diet with insects. The pale green, hollow leaf, 2 to 3 feet tall, attracts such prey as wasps, bees, ants, flies, and beetles. Veined with red or purple and dotted with clear, windowlike false exits, the domed leaf somewhat resembles a striking cobra.

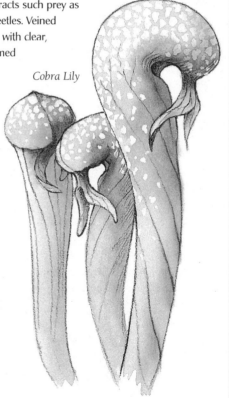

Cobra Lily

Partly covering the opening to the dome is a red and green fishtail-shaped structure that lures insects with nectar. On it, hairs direct the prey into the dome, where nectar glands intermingle with long, stiff hairs. These keep the insects moving farther inside the leaf, where slick surfaces and hairs speed the victim's descent into a pool of lethal broth secreted inside the base of the leaf. There, bacteria digest soft body parts, and plant walls absorb the nutrients.

• TRILLIUM •

The Northwest announces "Spring!" by the emergence in February of the trillium *(Trillium ovatum)*. This relative of lilies and grasses flaunts a large, three-petaled white blossom on a short stalk above a whorl of three broad, pointed leaves 5 inches long. Leaves as first curled around the emerging flower bud, gradually unfold. Trilliums brighten coniferous woods of western lowlands and wooded mountains in much of the Northwest. As the petals age, they turn pinkish. Ants carry away seeds, eating only the fatty part of one end. Thus the seeds germinate far from the plants.

The Makahs pounded the bulbs and rubbed them on the body as a love potion. Women added bulbs while cooking for potential lovers.

colored bract—a modified, petal-like leaf—encloses the clublike flower stalk crowded with hundreds of small, green, true flowers. Skunk cabbage often grows in swampy lowlands and in coastal forests.

All parts of the plant contain long-needled calcium oxalate crystals. The chemical compound temporarily paralyzes the salivary glands and causes throat and tongue to swell, impairing breathing. But bears eat the entire plant without ill effects, and elk, deer, and mountain beavers browse the peppery leaves.

Native Americans steamed or roasted the spathes and roots for several days before eating them, and dried the root to grind into flour. They used the leaves for berry and water containers, and for wrapping camas bulbs. Heated leaves soothed headaches and fevers, and were applied, along with spathes, as poultices for insect bites, boils, and rheumatic fever.

KELP

Few areas in the world top Northwest waters for number of marine algae (seaweed) genera and species (600), and for profuse growth of individual algae. Credit the rocky ocean bottom to attach holdfasts; the temperate climate; and cold, shallow water with high salinity and good water movement.

Brown algae, such as kelp, rank among the most complex of marine algae, with the highest tissue differentiation. Kelp thrives in Puget Sound, the San Juan Islands, and Washington's outer coast. Kelp is scarcer in Oregon waters because of hungry sea urchins and sandy ocean bottom.

Kelp forests break the force of destructive waves and currents on shorelines. In sheltered waters, stipes grow only to 20 feet; in subtidal open ocean they can reach 100 feet. The fist-sized holdfast anchors the kelp.

Bull kelp (*Nereocystis luetkeana*) holds world ranking for achieving the most elongated growth in a single season. A single stipe begins to grow in the spring, attached by a holdfast as deep as 60 feet. It increases up to 100 feet long, broadening to a gas-filled bulb 6 to 8 inches in diameter. Two groups

> **In sheltered waters, kelp stipes grow only to 20 feet; in subtidal open ocean they can reach 100 feet.**
>
> ●

of strap-shaped, golden brown fronds emerge from the bulb. Stipe and bulb float 32 to 64 tough blades up to 12 feet long and 5 inches wide.

The perennial giant kelp (*Macrocystis integrifolia*) grows profusely for several years, each plant sending forth several repeatedly branched stipes with hundreds of floats, each small globe supporting a single leaf 1 to 2 feet long. Giant kelp fronds absorb critical mineral salts, catch sunlight for photosynthesis, and move nutrients down to parts of the plant too deep to manufacture food. The multilevel kelp canopy offers shelter and food to many animals.

Coastal tribes such as the Makah used the large bull kelp globe to store water and fish oil. They dried kelp for winter food, flaking it off like chipped beef. The strong, flexible stipes, dried and oiled, made sturdy fishing lines for cod and halibut. Makah children played at harpooning whales with the long stipes, which also provided tiny wheels for toy wagons. (See Otters)

LICHENS

The odd couple—that's the biologically unique lichen. Two very different plants, an alga and a fungus, form a new compound, one that can reproduce by fragmentation. Each partner contributes to the union without harming the other. The fungus protects the alga from injury, drying out, and excessive exposure to sunlight while contributing moisture and minute amounts of minerals extracted from the air or substratum. The alga shares the food it makes by photosynthesis.

Lacking true roots, stems, leaves, vascular system, and chlorophyll, lichens are not true plants, although they have some plantlike structures. Most lichens are epiphytes, with a few of them

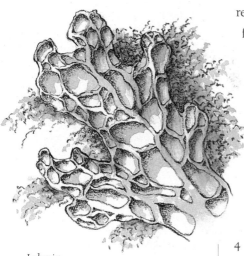

Lobaria

require 8 to 10 years to form fruiting bodies. Foliose lichens such as *Lobaria oregana* take 50 years to form a leathery "cabbage leaf" on a bigleaf maple. Most dramatic are the Usneas—"old man's beard." Many-branched and free-growing, without the threadlike roots of crustose lichens, they can grow to 3 or 4 feet long.

Lichens have long been used by humans and animals for food, dyes, and medicines. Lobaria fixes nitrogen in the soil as rain percolates through the lichens. The irony is that lichens, which survive temperatures from below freezing to 434°F, can be killed by air pollution. (See Epiphytes)

parasitic on mosses, or saprophytic on wood and bark.

The Pacific Northwest hosts several hundred lichen species in a variety of habitats—from coastal rain forests to salt-spray-washed ocean cliffs to arid deserts. All three main types of lichens are slow-growing, chalking up an inch or less a year. Crustose lichens disintegrate rock, using an acid secreted by fungal threads to penetrate 1/2 inch deep and begin the soil-making process. Even the faster-growing fruticose lichens

MUSHROOMS

Some mushrooms are delectable (chanterelles); others are deadly (amanitas). Most are the above-ground fruiting bodies of a below-ground network of fungus—the mycelium. They are neither plant nor animal.

The Pacific Northwest, with its temperate climate, seasonal rain, and large, moist coastal forests, ranks as a world center of mushroom diversity, with more than 3,000 species of fruiting fungi. The Pacific Northwest interior yields mushrooms in drier woods and such national forests as the Wallowa-Whitman in northeastern Oregon.

Mushrooms erupt only after the fungus has absorbed enough food from the soil, and when temperature and moisture are adequate, often after the first autumn rains. The mushroom's function is to scatter millions of microscopic spores. After a few days above ground, mushrooms deteriorate, and wind and animals disperse the spores. Mushrooms are a vital source of nutrients for animals; they concentrate 30 to 100 times more potassium, phosphorus, and nitrogen in their flesh than is available in foliage.

Ideal conditions in the damp forests west of the Cascades

Chanterelles

• THE WEB OF LIFE •

The idea of a networking web spreading out for mutual benefit dates back at least 400 million years. Mycorrhizal fungi, which form mutually beneficial relationships with green plants, keep trees in Pacific Northwest forests healthy and huge. Not every fungus is mycorrhizal, but 95 percent of most green plants, from orchids to cedars, depend upon at least one fungus. When a forest is cut, the fungi die with the trees.

Fungi lack organs such as leaves, roots, and stems. They also lack chlorophyll and the ability to manufacture their own food through photosynthesis. By linking up with green plants, they obtain sugars from the host in exchange for increasing the feeding area of its roots up to 2,000 times. This allows more efficient extraction of nutrients and water from the soil; some fungi even contribute antibiotics to protect host plants.

This work is done by the mycelium, the "body" of the fungus, which consists of a network of threadlike filaments called hyphae. The hyphae work with nitrogen-fixing bacteria in the root nodules, adjusting resources according to need for water or nutrients. An acre of forest can yield 2 1/2 tons of hyphae, dry weight. When conditions are right, the mycelium sends up spore-bearing, fruiting bodies—mushrooms. Although the hyphae modify the host roots, they never harm the host.

make Washington and Oregon the nation's largest producers of yellow and white chanterelle mushrooms (*Cantharellus cibarius* and *C. subalbidus*). The popular mushrooms are abundant in the Northwest because their preferred habitat is abundant: tall, second-growth Douglas fir and hemlock forests. The flesh of the funnel or vase-shaped apricot-orange chanterelles, with their distinctive vertical ridging on the stems, is relished for its meaty texture and nutty flavor.

Inland areas of the Pacific Northwest bear prolific crops of very large mushrooms such as the boletes, which bear pores instead of gills. The king bolete

(*Boletus edulis*) is the choicest—spongy with a sweet, nutty taste and pleasant aroma. Boletes grow on a stout stem on the floor of inland coniferous forests. Those of record size measure 12 inches across the smooth, reddish brown cap and can weigh 10 pounds.

Most puffballs (*Calvatia gigantea*) are only an inch or so across, but one weighing 21 pounds was found in 1992 on Washington's Olympic Peninsula near Sequim. Pine groves in Oregon's Winema and Deschutes National Forests account for 8 percent of the world's supply of costly matsutakes, a highly prized edible mushroom. Coral mushrooms, perennials that grow in a shaggy mass on the ground, can be harvested repeatedly.

Oregon boasts a white truffle (*Tuber gibbosum*) reminiscent of a rare Italian white truffle. These fruiting bodies remain underground around the roots of certain trees, especially oak.

Producing the truffles underground protects them from heat, drought, and frost, and avoids the uncertainties of wind dispersal of spores. That process is totally dependent upon the animals that eat the truffles. Very slow-growing, and often less than 2 1/2 inches across, the knobby truffles rely on a very intense odor (redolent of garlic, cheese, and spice) to help animals find them. (See Diets to Die For; The Web of Life)

SPHAGNUM MOSS

Forget the false mosses: reindeer, Irish, club. Sphagnum moss is a true moss that grows in many Pacific Northwest shallow ponds, wetlands, bogs, swamps, and undeveloped peatlands. All peat mosses belong to the genus *Sphagnum*.

Tremendous amounts of peat exist in the Pacific Northwest in areas covered by ice-age glaciers. Bogs are often kettle lakes: bowl-

Sphagnum Moss

shaped depressions in which a huge mass of ice from the retreating glacier was buried. When the mass melted, it left behind a depression tens of feet deep. Sphagnum moss grows best in wet climates warm enough for the moss to grow, cool enough to slow down decomposing bacteria. In cold northern waters, where decomposition is slow, peat piles up in silt from streams, filling in lake margins and bottomlands.

The dominant plant in poorly drained wet areas, sphagnum moss can grow for years because it is rootless. It extends its mat from the margins into the center of the pond, and downward about 4 feet, acidifying the water and forming a peaty turf. Only the light, springy living tops of the moss keep growing. After thousands of years, sphagnum moss completely fills small pools, which become thick enough for acid-loving plants to grow; their interlocked roots firm up the wetland.

Sphagnum moss can absorb nearly 20 times its own weight through the porous walls of very large leaf and stem cells. You can easily squeeze water out of it. Moss stays small because it cannot transport nutrients and moisture very far. Where humidity is high, however, strands of sphagnum moss can reach an astonishing 12 inches long.

One of the most dramatic bogs in the Pacific Northwest is covered with carnivorous cobra lilies near Florence, Oregon. Bogs are notoriously nitrogen-poor. So the pitcher-plant cobras trap insects and small reptiles to supplement their diets. One of the largest peat deposits in Washington, 82 feet deep and nearly 6,000 years old, comprises Mercer Slough in Bellevue. When the level of Lake Washington was lowered in 1916 during construction of the ship canal, much of the lake shoreline was exposed in sloughs of muck and peat. With low population on the east side, little development occurred there until World War II. Mercer Slough remained a boggy inlet with the vegetation of a true wetland. A number of plants have adapted to the special conditions of bogs: Labrador-tea, wild cranberry, bog blueberry, bog laurel. Even some coniferous trees grow in bogs, adapting by dwarfing. Bellevue fought later efforts to develop the land, and now the slough and peatland with abundant sphagnum moss are preserved as a city park.

Once peat, a valuable additive to garden soils, was mined in Washington, but the moss is no longer considered a replaceable resource. It grows very slowly, even when undisturbed. But eventually every body of water in the Pacific Northwest will fill in and become land. The bog is the transitional stage. Already Puget Sound has lost several estuaries, which have become fertile farmland. (See It's the Water; Epiphytes; Carnivorous Plants)

· T H R E E ·

N A T U R A L   F E A T U R E S

NATURAL FEATURES

Picture these natural extravaganzas of the Pacific Northwest: A black, bleak, dark-side-of-the-moon-scape littered with lava bombs, caves, and spatter cones. A jagged mountain skyline with sawtooth peaks of granite. A marble cave with glistening stalactites in fanciful forms. A blown-out volcano once Washington's most symmetrical peak. A clear, deep, peacock blue lake in a caldera more than 4 miles across. Columns of basalt standing like palisades in the walls of a great coulee. Oregon, Idaho, and Washington offer hundreds of such natural landscapes. They are evidence of upheaval: eruptions, mountains rising, enormous floods of lava and water.

The Pacific Northwest has known many such events, which have left their records on mountainsides, deep in canyons, and even high on mountain peaks. Rocks in all three Pacific Northwest states speak of ancient island arcs that traveled eastward thousands of miles across the sea on oceanic plates, destined to collide with the west-moving, ancient North American continent, very near Idaho's current boundary. Rocks tell us of relationships between the Blue Mountains in northeastern Oregon/southeastern Washington and the North Cascades in northernmost Washington, between coral that fringed those ancient islands and remains as limestone in a number of mountains.

The Pacific Northwest states are inextricably bound by climate, with Idaho cut off from maritime moisture to the west, but protected by the

Rockies from the harsh continental climate to the east. West of the Cascades, both Oregon and Washington enjoy temperate climates moderated by moisture from the Pacific, but at the expense of the interior, where the little moisture that arrives sustains mainly sagebrush and greasewood. Idaho would be much more arid except for its many mountain ranges, with 42 peaks higher than 10,000 feet. They capture enough precipitation during the winter to pile up huge snowdrifts that release water gradually during the summer, watering several thousand species of wildflowers.

The biogeographic provinces of the Northwest are distinctive and varied. Some are so huge they transcend state boundaries, most notably the Columbia Plateau (more properly called a basin), which encompasses parts of Washington, Oregon, and Idaho. The Snake River has carved Hells Canyon through several thousand feet of the plateau's thickly layered lava. Other provinces include the Puget–Willamette Trough and lowlands that stretch from British Columbia to Southern California, and that part of the Cascade Range extending from the Canadian border to Oregon's southernmost volcanoes.

In Washington, the Okanogan Highlands in the far northeastern corner and the Olympics in the far northwestern corner are distinct provinces. Oregon has its Coast Range and Pacific shore, its High Lava Desert, part of the basin and range province (which extends east into Idaho), and the Klamath Mountains. Idaho's provinces include lush northern mountain and lake country and, to the south, its barren eastern Snake River plain. The northeastern Selkirk Rrange—an outlier of the Northern Rockies—straddles northern Idaho and northeastern Washington.

Seeing it all would take three lifetimes.

BEACHES

Surf's up! The world's only driftwood beaches occur on the Pacific Northwest coast and Washington's Puget Sound. Driftwood—distinctive heaps of silvery, weathered logs and roots— piles up on saltwater beaches only where many large trees grow near the water, and only where the prevailing winds push floating objects toward shore, where they strand.

Most originates locally. Saw-logs escape from storage and towing booms in Puget Sound or the Columbia River and are carried out to sea, later washing up on ocean beaches. Most drift logs wash up during calm weather, but others can become battering rams when wave-propelled ashore during a storm.

Driftwood stabilizes beaches, forming natural traps for sand in which vegetation can grow. Piled several feet high, the stranded logs form a barrier to waves that erode cliffs and strip off beach sand.

Ocean beaches in northern Washington are scenic, with offshore stacks, arches, and islets, often accented by stunted, wind-shaped trees clinging to cliffs above pounding surf. Washington's sandy 28-mile-long Long Beach Peninsula, which

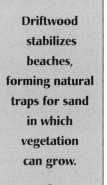

Driftwood stabilizes beaches, forming natural traps for sand in which vegetation can grow.

• MOUNTAINS CAST A LONG SHADOW •

The Westside Story: Rain, rain, go away. Topography in the Pacific Northwest has a tremendous influence on climate. High mountains create a barrier—a rain shadow—that forces water-saturated marine air to drop its moisture on the western side of the mountains. The air drops its water because, in rising to cross the mountain, it rapidly gets chilled in the higher altitude and can hold less water. Once it condenses that vapor, the air continues eastward. The mountains create a dry area where their shadow figuratively falls, influencing vegetation and rainfall. Because the Cascades run for some 700 miles, north and south, the eastern regions of Oregon and Washington are arid, with very low rainfall; sagebrush and lava plains prevail.

The Cascade rain shadow also affects Idaho. By the time marine air passes the mountains and crosses the Columbia Plateau, little moisture remains. Idaho's abundant water comes from high, snow-catching mountains, whose snow melts slowly in summer, filling rivers and watering northern forests. The Northern Rockies prevent most of the very cold, continental weather from the Great Plains from filtering through. Idaho does have many days over 100°F, but valleys are often temperate.

The Olympic rain shadow is small compared to that of the Cascades, but it affects the east side of the Olympic Peninsula, the north end of Whidbey Island, and parts of the San Juan Islands. The city of Sequim, not far as the raven flies from the rain-splashed ocean towns, is one of the driest coastal regions north of San Diego, averaging only 16 inches of rain a year.

shelters Willapa Bay from waves and wind, ranks as the longest natural expanse of unbroken ocean sand in the nation.

Swollen ice-age rivers and streams brought a variety of minerals to the southern Oregon coast, from Cape Blanco to Cape Arago. Streams still bring small amounts of valuable metals such as gold, platinum, and chromite to the coast, where ocean waves sort each by weight into curving swash marks. (See Oregon Coast; Olympic Mountains; Gem Minerals; All That Glitters)

BITTERROOT MOUNTAINS

Ruggedly handsome, the Bitterroot Range extends 300 miles along the middle border of Idaho and Montana, its peaks averaging 9,000 feet. Its highest is Scott Peak, 11,393 feet. Part of the Rocky Mountains, the Bitterroots' higher levels, which have been strongly glaciated with many cirques and U-shaped valleys, contain dense forests, steep canyons, high alpine meadows, and mountain lakes. The eastern slope is abrupt, a fault scarp. The range drains to the Columbia River via Clark Fork River on the east and Clearwater Salmon on the west.

Formerly, Native American tribes, including women and children, crossed the mountains every year to hunt buffalo on the eastern plains. The Lewis and Clark Expedition spent nine brutally exhausting days climbing to the crest of the range. They followed a Nez Perce trail located along ridgetops because of the inaccessible, steep-walled canyons. The expedition found the trail almost impassable, clogged with rocks and blown-down trees. By the time they found a Nez Perce camp down on the Weippe Prairie, the men were sick and almost starved. On the return trip, the expedition had the help of three Nez Perce guides. The men bathed in the hot springs still flowing at Lolo Pass, 5,233 feet high.

The Bitterroot Mountains were the scene of one of the West's worst forest fires. In the summer of 1910, thousands of individual fires blazed across the entire Bitterroot Range for more than two months. Three million acres were burned before rain dampened the fires.

BLUE AND WALLOWA MOUNTAINS

"The Alps of Oregon," the compact, ruggedly beautiful granite peaks of the Wallowa Mountains, rise in the northeastern corner of Oregon. A tramway/ gondola soars from Wallowa Lake nearly 4,000 feet in 15 minutes, one of the longest and steepest in the nation. It stops at the summit of 8,250-foot Mount Howard, with panoramic views of Wallowa Lake and Valley.

The highest peaks in the Blue Mountain geological province are in the Wallowas, to the east of the Blue Mountains. They lie within the Wallowa Terrane, largest remnant of the ancestral Blue Mountains volcanic island arc that once lay thousands of miles out in the Pacific. Below several thousand feet of Columbia Plateau lava lie ancient sedimentary and ocean crust rocks 250 million to 75 million years old, once part of that volcanic arc.

Rocks in the North Cascades and San Juan Islands are similar to many in the Blue Mountains and Wallowa Terrane. When the terranes were accreted to the North American shoreline, they became part of the Oregon coastline. The Wallowa Mountains overlook Hells Canyon to the east, where the Snake River forms much of the Idaho–Oregon boundary.

The Blue and Wallowa Mountains are the best known of a group of subranges that include Ochoco, Strawberry, Greenhorn, and Elkhorn, all greatly uplifted and separated by faulted basins and valleys. Heavily timbered Eagle Cap Wilderness, one of Oregon's most remote wilderness areas, encompasses a good part of the Wallowa Mountains. The wilderness is noted for deep river canyons cut by swift rivers, and for mountain peaks nearly 10,000 feet high.

> **A tramway soars from Wallowa Lake nearly 4,000 feet in 15 minutes, one of the longest and steepest in the nation.**
>
> ●

More accessible than the Wallowas, the Blues boast the Blue Mountain Scenic Byway along the summit of the 190-mile-long mountains. In the northern Blue Mountains, the Umatilla National Forest reaches into the southeast corner of Washington with its highest point, 8,131 feet. Wenaha-Tucannon Wilderness, which spans the Oregon–Washington border, is known for its rugged ridges and steep canyons, and for dedicated Sasquatch hunters. (See Hells Canyon and the Snake River; North Cascade Mountains)

CASCADE VOLCANOES

Beautiful—and potentially dangerous: The magnificent Cascade volcanoes are the high points of the Cascade Range, 700 miles long and 30 to 80 miles wide. Most northerly of the Cascade volcanoes in the United States is Mount Baker; most southerly of the Pacific Northwest's is Oregon's Mount McLoughlin. Part of the Pacific Ring of Fire, the volcanoes are comparatively young, built between 2 million and 25,000 years ago. The range boasts 19 peaks more than 9,000 feet high.

The Pacific Northwest's highest mountain, Mount Rainier was built upon the eroded shoulders of a Western Cascades volcano 40 million years old. At 14,411.1 feet, it ranks as the 5th-highest peak in the Lower 48, and the highest volcano. Mount Rainier bears the largest number of glaciers of any single peak in the Lower 48, totaling 36 square miles of perennial ice and snow.

Reaching so high into the upper atmosphere, Rainier intercepts the eastward flow of moist maritime air. Paradise Meadow, at 5,400 feet elevation, receives 620 inches of snow a year; Rainier holds the national record for the most snow recorded in a year. The summit is subject to subzero temperatures, winds of up to 100 miles an hour, rockfalls, rock slides, and avalanches. Its last eruption, primarily ash and pumice, occurred only 150 years ago. Since the last ice age, Rainier has produced 55 lahars—superheated landslides. The Osceola mudflow of 5,700 years ago collapsed Rainier's summit and lowered the mountain by 1,500 feet.

Rainier's rim and two summit craters are punctured by fumaroles emitting hot sulfurous gases. Surface temperature on the rim can reach 176°F. The western crater, 1,000 feet across, contains an underground lake at 14,000 feet. Under the summit icecap, steam jets and fumaroles have melted out steep-walled, high-ceilinged corridors at least a mile long. Mount Rainier, Mount Baker, and Alaska's Mount Wrangell are the only volcanoes to have hollowed out such tunnels. Rainier is now considered the most dangerous of the Cascade volcanoes.

Over thousands of years, Oregon's highest mountain, 11,239-foot Mount Hood, has let loose with hot ash, mudflows, lava flows, and debris avalanches. Unlike most other Cascade volcanoes, Hood was built largely of pyroclastic materials. At its maximum, it was perhaps 12,000 feet high.

Hood's last major eruption of lava came 15,000 years ago, with lava layers 500 feet thick from a crater on the southwest flank. Near its summit, Oregon's largest fumarole fields are intensely hot, evidence that the volcano is not extinct. The clouds often seen over the mountain are condensations of vapor or acidic gases smelling pungently of hydrogen sulfide gas. Those gases turn nearby rock to clay, increasing the potential for mudflows.

What were you doing on May 18, 1980, at 8:31 A.M. when the largest volcanic eruption in the recorded history of the Lower 48 states beheaded Mount St.

Helens? This first U.S. eruption since 1917 was one of the most powerful ever recorded by humans. Within seconds Mount St. Helens lost 1,320 feet of its symmetrical cone, dropping from Washington's 5th-highest mountain (9,677 feet) to

Mount Rainier

30th (8,364 feet). Scientists' experiences with much-monitored Mount St. Helens, now a national monument, have helped scientists all over the world understand how volcanoes behave between eruptions. From time to time steam billows out, ash and rocks are coughed up, and small earthquakes recur.

Washington's oldest and second-highest mountain,12,276-foot-high Mount Adams, is the only volcano to straddle the Cascade Divide. On the western slopes swordfern thrives; on the eastern side, sagebrush grows. Hydrogen sulfide gas on its summit can be smelled 6 miles away. Little is known about the history of the massive volcano, not even when it last erupted. The eastern slope is the most precipitous, with dangerous icefalls. Klickitat Glacier on the east side is second in size among Cascade glaciers only to Mount Rainier's Emmons. The summit icefield bears a cap of ice 210 feet deep. (See Glaciers; North Cascade Mountains; Waterfalls; Wet and Wild; Volcanoes Ancient and Modern)

CAVES

The longest unbroken lava tube cave in the Lower 48 lies in a lava flow from Washington's Mount St. Helens. Ape Cave stretches for 12,810 feet along the volcano's southern slope, tunneling through a lava flow nearly two millennia old. It survived the 1980 eruption. Most tube caves have only one level; Ape Cave has two. Among its varied formations—lava falls, floor ripples, tubular and ribbon stalactites—is a large lava ball wedged between two walls about 10 feet above the floor.

A few lava tube caves contain permanent ice (lava rock is an efficient insulator). Winter temperatures outside must be very cold; dense, chilled air sinks to the bottom of the cave. Idaho's Shoshone Indian Ice Caves, inside a lava tube 3 miles long, are the most accessible of such ice caves in the Snake River Plain. The complex system of twisted lava, arched bridges, deep pits, and potholes covers 80 square miles with both roofed and unroofed tubes. The air inside the ice caves is a wintry 18°F to 28°F, even when summer temperatures outside rise to more than 100°F. The solid ice floor, 1,000 feet long, is nearly 30 feet thick. A wall of ice measures 40 feet high and 20 feet wide.

The Sea Lion Caves north of Florence on the Oregon coast rank as the world's largest natural sea cave: 310 feet long, 165 feet wide, and 50 feet high. The floor area of the vaulted main chamber covers nearly an acre. Steller sea lions and seabirds use the largest of its three entrances, facing west.

Most limestone caves form as slightly acidic groundwater percolates through sedimentary

> **Oregon Caves National Monument in south-central Oregon is the largest West Coast cave formed of marble.**
>
> ●

rock that is largely calcium carbonate. Drop by drop, over tens of thousands of years, highly mineralized water drips from chamber ceilings to form stalactites, splashes onto the floor to form stalagmites, and flows over ledges and down walls to form draperies and cascades.

One of the few large limestone caverns in Idaho, at the highest altitude of any Northwest limestone cave, penetrates the Wasatch Mountains in southeastern Idaho. Minnetonka Cave, with its entrance at 7,700 feet above sea level, has nine chambers—one 300 feet wide and 90 feet high—with beautiful displays of banded travertine rock ("cave onyx"), numerous stalactites and stalagmites, and ice crystals clinging to walls. Embedded in the cave limestone are fossilized prehistoric marine animals and plants.

Oregon Caves National Monument in south-central Oregon is the largest West Coast cave formed of marble. Folding and fracturing may have produced heat that softened limestone, with a searingly hot igneous intrusion recrystallizing the cave into pure marble. Oregon Caves, really a single cave, has five levels that include several miles of narrow passages and an underground stream. The largest chamber, the Ghost Room, measures 50 feet wide, 250 feet long, and 40 feet high. Cave formations, unusually varied for so small an area, include deposits resembling a cluster of bananas, a petrified garden, a chandelier, pillars, soda straws, and popcorn.

CITY OF ROCKS

A great place to visit, but no one ever lived in the silent City of Rocks National Reserve in southwestern Idaho's high desert. Oregon Trail travelers usually stopped there to rest and to gape at what appears to be, from a distance, an ancient ruined city. Thousands carved names and dates into Register Rock, or scrawled them with axle grease. These early travelers bestowed on the weirdly shaped rocks such names as Dragon's Head, Old Woman, and Bathtub Rock—a 200-foot-high rock with a concave top. The strangely beautiful formations are popular now with rock climbers, attracted by the quantity and variety of climbs.

The oddly shaped, eroded rocks, which resemble towers and turreted castles, tubs and bottles, pillars and spires, thrust up in the basin of a batholith dome of fine-grained, pinkish rhyolite. The batholith gradually cracked into blocks and pillars as water seeped into fractures during the very short rainy season in that arid region. Freezing and thawing also split the rock, forming monoliths, turrets, caves, and domes. Hoodoos— shaped by differential erosion of horizontal strata of varying hardness—may rise 250 feet.

A secondary "City of Rocks" formed of volcanic tuff is located near Gooding, Idaho, at an elevation of up to 6,200 feet, in hills abruptly uplifted in a block out of the Snake River plain. The fins, pillars, arches, and mushroom caps were also formed by differential weathering, penetration of water into fractures, and the freeze-and-split process. Obsidian chips are scattered throughout the welded tuff. This "city" includes one of the largest diatomaceous deposits in the nation, laid down when a huge, shallow lake covered the plain. (See Gem Minerals)

COLUMBIA RIVER

Most rivers go gently into that great ocean. Not the Columbia. Some 2,100 shipwrecks

> The strangely beautiful City of Rocks National Reserve is popular now with rock climbers, attracted by the quantity and variety of climbs.
>
> ●

have occurred there. At the river's mouth, the great tidal river current of the Columbia collides catastrophically with powerful Pacific Ocean waves that average 10 to 12 feet. At times easterly winds gust at 160 miles an hour. The channel at the river's shallow and unpredictable mouth, one of the world's three most treacherous, keeps changing.

The Northwest's longest and largest river flows 1,243 miles from its British Columbia source of Columbia Lake (2,650 feet in elevation) to its mouth. Six miles wide at Astoria, the Columbia ranks as the largest West Coast river to empty into the Pacific. The Columbia and its tributaries, a 259,000-square-mile watershed, comprise the principal river system of the Cascade Range, draining almost the entire chain. Once, the river boiled with

109 rapids and waterfalls. Now only one free-flowing stretch remains between Bonneville Dam and the Canadian border— 50-mile-long Hanford Reach.

The river has gouged out the Columbia River Gorge—the only significant break in the Cascade– Sierra Nevada mountain chain. The scenic and geologically interesting gorge varies from 5 to 8 miles wide and plunges 4,500 feet, with sheer cliffs and 77 waterfalls in 420 square miles.

The Columbia River Gorge encompasses two distinct biological and climatic regions. Western hemlock and Douglas fir heavily forest the Pacific end, giving way in the east to ponderosa pine and Garry oak. The rainfall at the Cascade Locks is 75 inches a year; at The Dalles, 14 inches. In the winter, dry, often bitterly cold air from the eastern interior collides with moist, warmer ocean air, causing blizzards and ice storms. Strong

Columbia River Gorge

high-pressure systems east of the Cascade Range can bring gale-force easterly winds through the gorge. But the narrower parts of the gorge funnel wind through at a steady 15 to 25 miles an hour—ideal for windsurfers.

The gorge provided a major route for plant and animal migration between the eastern and western regions of Washington and Oregon. The area boasts 73 species of butterflies, 22 species of ferns, and 1,000 plant species, (at least 6 endemic). In 1986 Congress formed the Columbia River Gorge National Scenic Area, which extends in Oregon from Troutdale in the west to The Dalles in the east, and in Washington from Washougal to Maryhill. (See Rivers; Columbia Flood Basalt Plateau; Missoula Floods)

CRATERS OF THE MOON

It looks like a wasteland, but in 83 square miles Idaho's Craters of the Moon National Monument displays more variety of young basaltic features than any other area its size in the Lower 48. The monument contains three kinds of basaltic lava: clinkery *a'a* lava; billowy, ropy, or wrinkled *pahoehoe* lava; and the rarer blocky lava, with smooth-faced, angular blocks 3 feet across. Most plentiful and colorful is the iridescent blue-green Blue Dragon flow, up to 45 feet thick. A unique cobalt blue flow features "squeeze-up" lava.

In what is now the northeast corner of Idaho's Snake River plain, at an elevation of 7,576 feet, eruptions dating from 15,000 to 2,100 years ago spilled millions of tons of lava onto thick lava of 5 million years before. These newest eruptions occurred along a 25-mile-long fissure of the Great Rift. Craters of the Moon includes some of the nation's most recent lava flows, relatively uneroded because of some years rainfall as low as 10 inches. Freezing and thawing, however, have created grotesque forms.

On display are natural bridges, 100 fumaroles, broad lava rivers atop other lava flows, and fragments of a crater wall standing upright like ruined trees (Devil's Orchard). Big Cinder Butte, nearly 800 feet high, is one of the few purely basaltic cinder cones in the region. Lava bombs 1/2 inch to 13 feet long, shaped like spindles, ribbons, or footballs, formed when blobs of lava flung into the air twisted and solidified as they fell. A tree mold section includes both standing and fallen trees up to 3 feet in diameter, encased in lava and burned out.

The monument also includes Indian Tunnel, a lava tube cave 830 feet long, and others up to 30 feet in diameter. Boy Scout Cave maintains its floor of ice even in summer. (See Great Rift)

DUNES

Living dunes? Yes, true dunes move, shifting with wind and season. Ripples in the sand indicate active dunes; constant movement discourages vegetation. Oregon's coastal sand dunes—the nation's most extensive, active, ocean-related dunes—move up to 18 feet a year, always in the direction of the prevailing wind—north and northwest in summer, 12 to 16 miles an hour. Winter winds from the south and southwest may gust to more than 100 miles an hour in a severe storm. Both wind and water—tides, currents, and waves—have created sand and shaped the dunes.

The best-known dune area stretches along the Oregon coast for 55 miles, sometimes extending inland nearly 4 miles. The 40-mile-long Oregon Dunes National Recreation Area lies between Coos Bay and Florence. Oregon's dunes are among the tallest coastal dunes in the world, averaging 250 feet high, with oblique dunes sometimes rising more than 500 feet. Oblique dunes, angled to the wind, are the most active, often forming narrow parallel ridges. Transverse dunes are lower, 5 to 20 feet high, forming wavelike dunes perpendicular to the direction of the wind.

The tallest landlocked sand dune in North America, rising 470 feet, soars in Bruneau Dunes State Park in southwestern Idaho within the Birds of Prey National Conservation Area. That large active dune, along with an overlapping dune, covers 16 acres. The Bruneau dunes are unique in the western hemisphere in rising not at the edge but from the center of their natural sandy basin. The pepper-and-salt dunes—with sand coming from black basalt and white quartz—are barchan (crescent) dunes hundreds of feet long. Inland dunes often are crescent-shaped, with the wind, which never changes direction, forming long "horns" downwind.

Some of Washington's largest and most active inland dunes

> **The tallest landlocked sand dune in North America, rising 470 feet, is in Idaho.**
>
> ●

have accumulated in the state's smallest wilderness area. Juniper Dunes Wilderness protects an area of more than 7,000 acres near Pasco, with dunes rising to 130 feet and ranging in width from 200 to 1,200 feet. Washington's greatest concentration of western juniper trees reaches its northernmost limits in these dunes, with rainfall of 12 inches a year.

ESTUARIES

A bridge made of water? An estuary, which bridges land and sea, mingles freshwater with seawater, blending the nutrients each carries. Some estuaries produce 20 times as much food for marine creatures as the same area of open sea. An estuary is always changing, altering salinity, water temperature, and sediment deposition, aided by wind and twice-a-day tides. Estuaries often occur in a long arm reaching

• MESSAGES FROM THE UNDERGROUND •

Put an ear to the ground near Idaho's Snake River Plain Aquifer, and you can, so it's said, hear water running. That aquifer, 3,000 feet deep, is one of the world's greatest. Extending almost 100 miles northeast from Hagerman Valley, it holds hundreds of times more water than any of Idaho's surface reservoirs, making it one of the state's most valuable resources.

Water that flows off central Idaho's lofty mountain ranges, which receive heavy winter precipitation, drains into the nearby lava plain, which is porous and deeply fissured by faults. Thousands of years ago, rivers such as Big Lost River and Little Lost River flowed aboveground to join the Snake River, but repeated lava flows filled in their channels, compelling them to cut new ones. Lava flows forced even the Snake River into a great curve to the southwest. For 268 miles downstream from the junction of Henry's Fork River and the Snake, not one perennial stream joins the Snake from the north. Unable to maintain their channels, the rivers went underground, fueling the aquifer.

The movement of subterranean water is aided by the downwarping of the plain, due in part to the enormous weight of lava and water. After traveling more than 100 miles, the water finally emerges as springs cascading down the steep canyon walls along the north bank of the Snake River. There they gush out at nearly 600 cubic feet a second. Each year, those springs add 200 billion cubic feet of much-needed water to an almost dry Snake River below Milner Dam. For 94 miles downstream from the dam, no water flows during maximum diversion for irrigation—not until the springs renew the river.

The Spokane Valley–Rathdrum Prairie Aquifer is part of a regional groundwater system that includes parts of northern Idaho's Panhandle and eastern Washington. Spokane Valley's 350,000 people depend upon this aquifer, one of the nation's most efficient alluvial-type aquifers. Its sedimentary deposits, 400 to 700 feet thick, were laid down by the many Missoula floods. Coarse gravel, common alongside rivers, is highly porous, able to store large amounts of groundwater that actively recharge such aquifers. Smaller aquifers abound throughout the Pacific Northwest. (See Springs) inland from the sea, or in a partly enclosed bay, with highly productive mudflats and wetlands with abundant phytoplankton to feed numerous and diverse marine creatures, both residents and migrants.

Of Oregon's 15 small estuaries, Yaquina Bay is the fourth largest at 4,200 acres; tidal water reaches 10 miles upriver. Smaller Oregon estuaries, such as Netart Bay in the Tillamook area, may be marine dominated, with too much tidal water for the small amount of freshwater. The South Slough of Coos Bay estuary encompasses 600 acres of tidal marshes, mudflats, and open water channels leading to the ocean. The first national estuarine sanctuary, established there in 1974, harbors shellfish and small animals.

Four of the five major estuaries on the West Coast are located in Washington waters: Padilla Bay, Skagit Bay, Willapa Bay, and—the grandfather of them all—Puget Sound, one of the largest, deepest estuaries in the nation. Willapa Bay, located in Washington's extreme southwestern corner, is the most pristine coastal estuary in the Lower 48. Long Beach Peninsula, 20 miles long and 1 mile wide, almost completely shields the bay from rough Pacific waters.

Willapa Bay is one of the West Coast's most productive estuaries, with Dungeness crab; chinook, chum, and coho salmon; and English sole, plus 15,000 acres of oysters and clams. At low tide, nearly half the bottom of Willapa Bay is exposed, with 44,000 acres of mudflats, a quarter of the productive shellfish-growing waters of the western United States. Its extensive salt marsh supports a host of wildlife, including migratory birds for which it provides the largest feeding habitat in the Pacific Flyway.

Unfortunately, a fast-spreading cordgrass dominant in East Coast salt marshes, *Spartina alterniflora*, has recently become invasive, threatening prime oyster beds. It has almost reached Canadian waters. In 50 years it could cover two-thirds of all the intertidal bay, creating sandbars, causing shoaling, and blocking the outgoing tide. Another potential disaster, the European green crab, is settling in. An aggressive predator that can open crab, oyster, clam, and mussel shells, it grows twice its normal size—to 3 inches—in Pacific Northwest waters and seems capable of learning. It may have floated up from San Francisco or arrived in ballast water dumped here. (See Greater Puget Sound)

GLACIERS

Can't take the pressure? Be glad you're not a glacier. Glacial ice is created by accumulating, compacting, and recrystallizing snow. When the new ice is about 100 feet thick, the glacier starts oozing out from the margins of snow- and icefields.

Small, high alpine glaciers (also called mountain glaciers) begin when ice grinds into a mountain, gouging out a cirque. Valley glaciers, which exist today only in Alaska, are formed when an alpine glacier descends into a valley and fills it with ice, creating the classical U-shaped glacial valley. As it flows over uneven ground, the top begins to crack—sign of an active glacier.

Glaciers are one of the most powerful forces of erosion, grinding rock into fine "rock flour." Both Mount Hood and Mount Rainier have lost thousands of tons of material to glacial erosion; little of Rainier's original surface remains.

In mountainous Idaho, where $9/10$ of the state's surface is covered with mountains, there are no permanent glaciers even though seven peaks soar to over 12,000 feet and trap a heavy load of snow in the winter. The snow melts before it can become a glacier.

Washington's volcanoes boast by far the most extensive network of glaciers in the Lower 48—135 square miles. Most of the nation's active glaciers outside Alaska lie on the higher ridges of the Cascade and Olympic Mountains. Mount Olympus, only 7,965 feet, has 7 glaciers. Mount Baker, 10,788 feet, is, like Mount Olympus, near enough to the sea to capture 200 inches of precipitation that feed its glaciers. Mount St. Helens, which lost nearly 75 percent of its glaciers in its 1980 eruption, recently revealed a crevassed icefield within the crater—that spells glacier.

The North Cascades contain 750 glaciers from Canada to Snoqualmie Pass and Puget Sound to the Columbia River. North Cascades National Park alone holds 318 glaciers, most quite small and retreating. During the last several decades, warmer winters have reduced the size of most of Washington's alpine glaciers. If the warming trend continues, many will vanish, particularly in the North Cascades, where only 60 glaciers have ideal conditions to survive.

Mount Rainier has 25 major named glaciers and 50 smaller ice patches. Nisqually Glacier, 4 miles long, ranks as one of the world's most accessible glaciers, reached by car and by foot. The first U.S. glacier to be documented (1857), it is the most-studied glacier in the western hemisphere. Photographs date back to 1884, and records of its size, to 1857. Rainier's longest and largest glacier is deeply crevassed Emmons, 5 miles long. Carbon Glacier, more than 4 1/2 miles long, contains the mountain's thickest ice—705 feet at 6,200 feet elevation. Carbon

> **Most of the nation's active glaciers outside Alaska lie on the higher ridges of the Cascade and Olympic Mountains.**

Glacier terminates at the lowest elevation of any glacier in the Lower 48: 3,200 feet. (See Volcanoes)

GRAND COULEE

It's really cool—a steep-sided trench that once carried the largest river of the Pacific Northwest. Grand Coulee is one of the world's most impressive examples of glacial and flood drainage; at its maximum it measures 900 feet deep, up to 5 miles wide at the northern end, and nearly 30 miles long. The coulee is actually two sections at different levels—Upper and Lower Grand Coulee, joined by Dry Falls. The entire chasm runs southwest for some 50 miles. For much of that length, the walls are sheer basalt with some of the Columbia Plateau's most imposing lava-shrinkage colonnades, 200 feet high, 3 feet in diameter, and a mile long.

The Columbia River didn't cut Grand Coulee unassisted, as geologists once believed. The river was joined by the ice-age Missoula floods. Together, racing along at up to 40 miles an hour, they scoured the coulee walls and floors of basalt lava and tore truck-sized chunks of basalt from the upper coulee's steep walls. The surging water also gouged caves in the lower part of Lower Coulee walls, and dumped great gravel bars across the plateau.

Another impressive coulee feature, Dry Falls, is an enormous dry waterfall, which was one of the world's largest waterfalls. It cut a gorge upstream from Soap Lake nearly 20 miles long. A similar waterfall within Upper Grand Coulee was 800 feet high and 1 1/2 miles wide at the downstream end. Massive Steamboat Rock, an 800-foot-high mesa inside upper Grand Coulee, is all that remains of that giant waterfall of that era. Lower Grand Coulee is punctured with small lakes, perhaps plunge pools for the ever-receding falls. Upper Coulee now hosts Banks

Steamboat Rock inside Upper Grand Coulee

Lake, 27 miles long and 100 feet deep, an "equalizing reservoir" for Grand Coulee Dam. (See Columbia River; Columbia Plateau Flood Basalt; Missoula Floods)

GREAT BASIN

Also called basin and range, the Great Basin is, in reality, not one basin but a series of small basins, each deeply filled with alluvial material and separated from one another by a series of north-south-running mountain ranges—solitary fault-block mountains. This unique natural province extends from southern Idaho to southern Utah and west through most of Nevada to southern Oregon. Snake River plain is such a basin, filled with several thousand feet of lava; the plain is still stretching as valleys widen. Idaho's highest peak, Mount Borah, at 12,662 feet, rises from a fault-block mountain, Big Lost River. The largest examples of Oregon's fault-block mountains, located in southeastern Alvord Desert, are Steens Mountain (the highest fault block in the nation, 9,733 feet), Abert Rim, and Hart Mountain.

A fault-block mountain is a single, mountain-sized chunk of the earth's crust bounded by faults and thrust up by movement along those faults; at the same time, the adjacent valley, or basin, drops, usually several times more than the mountain rises. Fault-block mountains rise gently on one side, and precipitously on the other (the fault scarp). The western side of Steens Mountain gains 5,000 feet in 20 miles; its eastern side reaches the same height in only 3 miles.

> **Fault block mountains rise gently on one side and precipitously on the other (the fault scarp).**
>
> ●

Basin and range country is always badly fractured by active faults, but most fault movement in Oregon's basin and range occurred long ago. During the destructive 1983 earthquake in Thousand Springs Valley, Borah Peak was uplifted 6 inches while the basin below dropped 4 feet.

The Great Basin is arid, with alkaline soil. At the base of Steens Mountain, rainfall is 7 inches a year; at the top, 32 inches. Climb to the summit and you pass through several ecological zones, from sagebrush to juniper to aspen to alpine meadows. Steens piles up 20 feet of snow in winter. A number of rivers drain the mountain.

The faults along which such mountains rise allow mineralized hot water to rise as hot springs. Steens and Hart Mountains are endowed with springs and shallow lakes. Hart's fault scarp, one of the highest in North America, rises some 3,000 feet above Warner Valley, 8,065 above sea level. Hart Mountain National Antelope Refuge supports more than 330 species of plants and animals, including pronghorn antelope. (See Pronghorn Antelope; Springs)

GREATER PUGET SOUND

Estuary? Fjord? Inland sea? By any name, Puget Sound forms one of the Northwest's most distinctive physical features.

From its northernmost reach at Admiralty Inlet, this long inland arm of the Pacific Ocean flows 55 miles to its southern tip at Commencement Bay. The Sound fills the largest, deepest glacier-sculpted basin in the Lower 48.

The Puget lowlands extend from British Columbia through the Willamette Valley to Oregon's Klamath Mountains. Formed by continental sediment accumulating for millions of years, this land buckled and lowered as the Olympic Mountains rose. After the last ice-age glacier receded, the land slowly rebounded. Salt water gradually filled the lowland trough, creating Puget Sound.

Puget Sound comprises four main interconnecting basins more than 600 feet deep and further subdivided. The flow of water between basins is hindered by underwater ridges called sills. The highest, at Admiralty Inlet where the Sound joins the Strait of Juan de Fuca, rises 218 feet.

In the Sound, colder, denser salt water flows in on the tides through the Strait and mixes with warmer, brackish freshwater from the 24 rivers and streams emptying into the Sound. Fast-moving currents through shallow inlets between islands aid the mixing. Water races through the Tacoma Narrows at 5.1 knots, and boils through Deception Pass at a daunting 8 knots maximum.

Along with freshwater, the rivers dump enormous amounts of sediment into the Sound. The ocean, too, contributes from its endless erosion of shores and cliffs. This abundance of sedimentary and organic matter will eventually fill the Puget Sound trough. Already bottom layers of sediment total 3,000 feet.

Hood Canal is the southernmost fjord on the western coast of North America. Although the canal is commonly thought of as part of Puget Sound, its southern end does not connect with the Sound. Its waters are considered continuous with those of the Strait of Juan de Fuca.

Before glaciation, it was a natural river valley, extending much farther south. During the Ice Age, the trough was deepened below sea level by the Puget Sound ice lobe. When the glacier withdrew, the river was drowned by salt water—a true fjord.

Hood Canal, whose trench is 500 to 600 feet deep, has long underwater walls and ledges. It is well populated with giant octopus, wolf-eels, crabs, sea urchins, sea anemones, and oysters. At the entrance to Hood Canal, currents are strong and water levels can vary up to 18 vertical feet a day. The highest waves on record for greater Puget Sound—8 feet—developed during a storm on Dabob Bay. Dabob Bay Natural Area Preserve at the bay's north end protects one of the best salt marshes remaining in the Puget Sound lowlands. (See Estuaries)

HELLS CANYON AND THE SNAKE RIVER

White-water heaven! Hells Canyon National Recreation Area contains the last primitive part of the Snake River, with 67 1/2 miles of it protected under the National Wild and Scenic Rivers Act. Rapids alternate with quiet stretches as the river often drops more than 11 feet a mile. Almost inaccessible, Hells Canyon, which forms the border between Oregon and Idaho for miles, is part of the Snake River Canyon. Hells Canyon is the deepest, most rugged river gorge in North America; for some 40 miles it averages 5,500 feet deep. It measures more than 7,900 feet to the highest peak of Seven Devils Mountains. This narrow range that separates the Snake and Salmon Rivers flanks Hells Canyon in Idaho; the Wallowas border it in Oregon.

The Snake River, Idaho's longest and the major tributary of the Columbia River, totals

1,038 miles. It gouged out the huge canyon through the western Snake River plain after the last layers of basalt lava were laid down some 13 million years ago. Like the Columbia River, the Snake cut through a rising mountain range, the Blue Mountains. Pushed east by the rising mountains, the river was forced to carve its canyon partly through very hard oceanic greenstone.

As the Snake River continues to carry eroded canyon rock into the Columbia, the load on the earth's crust lightens, causing the rims and mountains above the canyon to rise. Basalt that caps He-Devil Peak high above the

Hells Canyon

canyon—the highest Columbia Plateau basalt found anywhere—indicates major uplift. The erosion and uplift continue today.

Hells Canyon is so deep that several ecosystems exist within it. Summer air within the canyon can reach more than 120°F. Mild winter temperatures and horizontal basalt ledges outcropping in the upper walls prompted Native Americans and, later, European settlers to spend the cold months within the canyon, either in pit dwellings or in caves in the basalt walls.

ISLANDS

Islands, islands everywhere. Washington boasts the nation's largest saltwater island, the largest island in a Pacific Coast estuary, and the scenic, geologically intriguing San Juan archipelago. Idaho's lovely Coeur d'Alene Lake is island enhanced, and so is Oregon's Crater Lake. Both Oregon and Washington count numerous islandlike ocean rocks used by sea mammals and birds, but the vast majority of Pacific Northwest islands lie within greater Puget Sound. Lake Washington washes the shores of Mercer and Foster Islands.

At the north end of Puget Sound lies Whidbey Island, largest U.S. island surrounded by salt water, 48 miles long and 10 miles across at its widest. The island offers 200 miles of saltwater shoreline, with lagoons that attract waterfowl and migratory birds; eight lakes and four state parks; and Puget Sound's largest sand dunes. With freshwater and food plentiful, Native Americans lived there for thousands of years. Fire-cracked rocks, shell middens, and flaked obsidian stonepoints 6,000 years old are still found on Whidbey Island.

The San Juan Islands spread westward for 30 miles from the city of Anacortes on Fidalgo Island to the international boundary line in Haro Strait. Of the 768 rocks, reefs, islets, and

San Juan Islands

islands visible at low tide in the archipelago, only 475 of the largest are above water at high tide. Only 175 of the islands have been named. Some 86 islands from 0.02 to 140 acres in size comprise the San Juan Islands National Wildlife Refuge.

Orcas Island, larger than San Juan Island by only 1 1/2 square miles, is the coolest, wettest, and most mountainous of the archipelago, with Mount Constitution, the islands' highest peak at 2,409 feet. Orcas boasts the largest state park in the islands: 3,600 acres. The most weirdly beautiful islands in the group are the most northerly,

including the 11 rocks, reefs, and islets of weathered Chuckanut Formation sandstone that make up Sucia Island, 2 1/2 miles north of Orcas Island.

Both Oregon and Washington can claim a freshwater island in the Columbia: Oregon has Sauvie Island, 10 miles from Portland, near the confluence of the Columbia and Willamette Rivers, and Washington has Puget Island, a farming and residential island about 4 miles long. Sauvie Island, 15 miles long, may be the nation's largest island completely surrounded by freshwater. The many Sauvie Island lakes attract 250 species of birds, 37 species of mammals, and 12 species of amphibians and reptiles, including the rare painted turtle. Resident Native Americans called the island Wappatoo after potatolike tubers that grew there. Artifacts 2,000 years old have been found there.

Sauvie Island, 15 miles long, may be the nation's largest island completely surrounded by freshwater.

●

Long Island, 7 miles long and 2 miles wide, is the largest island in a Pacific Coast estuary (Willapa Bay). The island is part of the 11,000-acre Willapa National Wildlife Refuge, whose extensive eelgrass beds attract thousands of migrating black brant. One of the last remnants of an old-growth climax forest of cedars flourishes on Long Island. (See Sanctuaries at Sea)

LAKES

Thanks to the last ice age, the Pacific Northwest does not lack for lakes, even in arid country. In Washington, Spokane can boast of 76 lakes within 50 miles. In Oregon's high desert, remnants of once-large ancient lakes still remain: Silver, Christmas, and Fossil Lakes were once part of 100-foot-deep Fort Rock Lake. An ancient lake in Lake County once covered 461 square miles but shrank to Summer Lake and Lake Abert. A hot spring (170°F) issuing from the bottom of 10-acre Borax Lake in Alvord Basin keeps the temperature of Oregon's largest geothermal lake at 97°F, attracting trumpeter swans, snowy plovers, and other birds.

Largest, longest, deepest, and most scenic natural lake in Washington is Lake Chelan, which extends from the edge of the Columbia Plateau into the North Cascades near Glacier Peak. This fjordlike finger lake, carved by two glaciers, is more than 50 miles long, 1/4 to 2 miles wide, and

1,500 feet deep, third-deepest natural freshwater lake in the Lower 48.

In the high mountains of all three Northwest states, glaciers have created lovely alpine lakes. Volcano craters and calderas are ready-made basins for lakes: Pauline and East Lakes, once a single lake, lie within Newberry Caldera; Oregon's highest lake is cupped in a crater at the 10,358-foot summit of South Sister.

Queen of them all is Oregon's Crater Lake in the collapsed summit of Mount Mazama. The nation's deepest lake at 1,932 feet and the world's seventh deepest, Crater Lake has some of the clearest water in the world. Few plants can manufacture food in waters deeper than 200 feet because of limited light, but in Crater Lake a moss species thrives at 400 feet, the greatest known depth of any such moss in the world.

Idaho is justifiably proud of its three Panhandle lakes. A scenic 2-mile channel joins 19-mile-long Priest Lake and Upper Priest Lake, 3 miles long. Pend Oreille Lake, of glacial origin, is the second-largest natural lake west of the Mississippi: 43 miles long, 6 miles wide. It is also one of the nation's deepest at 1,100 feet deep. Coeur d'Alene Lake stretches for 25 miles and is indented by 24 bays. Some of the nation's largest flocks of ospreys winter at Coeur d'Alene Lake. But for some 100 years, the lake acted as a settling pond for 72 tons of toxic mine waste and mill tailings. The cost of restoration of lake, streams, groundwater, soil, wetlands, and other wildlife habitat dims the luster of all that gold. (See Newberry Caldera; Volcanoes Ancient and Modern; Gold)

MIMA MOUNDS

The final chapter has yet to be written in "The Mystery of the Mima Mounds." Few geological oddities in the

Northwest have been studied so intensively and still remain a mystery. Geologists shake their heads in puzzlement at Washington's multiple circular mounds that dot a grassy prairie near Olympia. From 1 to 7 feet high, and up to 70 feet in diameter (40 feet is more usual), the mounds consist of a random mix of silt, sand, and loam with gravel and small pebbles, resting on a base of coarse gravel deposited by meltwater from the Puget lobe of glacial ice. Near the center, the silt descends into the prairie gravel.

Similar mounds have been found elsewhere at the limits of glaciation and explained as the result of repeated freezing and thawing; however, such mounds also appear in frostless areas. Other theories center around

Mima Mounds

differential erosion by wind or water or wind-borne deposits surrounding trees or bushes. Whimsical explanations include buffalo wallows, anthills, shellfish feast remains, and nests made by prehistoric fish or pocket gophers. It is more likely that the Vashon Glacier, as it receded, left behind randomly sorted piles of gravel. Alternate freezing and thawing could then have cracked and bulged the piles, gradually forming mounds.

Plows, grazing cattle, and sand and gravel miners have taken their toll of the thousands of mounds. The 445-acre Mima Mounds Natural Area protects about 4,000 of the best. They are most impressive in the spring when covered with buttercups, violets, and shooting stars.

NEWBERRY CALDERA

Volcano lovers, get thee to Newberry National Volcanic Monument on the High Lava Plains in southeastern Oregon. There, many diverse volcanic formations spread out over hundreds of square miles. Newberry Caldera is more than 5 miles in diameter, almost as large as Crater Lake.

Newberry, a low-profile, shield volcano, with large base and gentle slopes, was active intermittently for only half a million years but was unusual in erupting four different kinds of lava. Its most recent activity occurred less than 2,000 years ago. The enormous magma chambers were drained by many lava flows from more than 400 parasitic basalt cinder cones 200 to 500 feet high that stud the volcano's slopes. All that remains of the walls of the 9,000-foot-high volcano after its summit collapsed is Paulina Peak, nearly 8,000 feet above sea level.

The aging volcano continued to erupt ash, pumice, and enormous obsidian flows. The most recent eruption, 1,350 years ago, produced Big Obsidian Flow, North America's most extensive and most recent. In its last cycle of eruption Newberry produced six separate obsidian flows, interlayered with pumice. The glossy, wrinkled obsidian ends in cliffs 100 feet high with a solidified cataract descending from a high vent. Minerals dissolved in Newberry obsidian color it black, brown, or red, sometimes gold-striped or with a gold or silver sheen. Native Americans more than 8,000 years ago traded weapons and tools chipped out of the obsidian.

The monument includes one of the world's largest, most symmetrical, and most accessible cinder cones (with a narrow road leading to its crater summit), Lava Butte, 500 feet above a jagged lava field. Youngest and northernmost of eight cones, the butte straddles huge Brothers Fault, one of the largest exposed faults in North America.

Lava Cast Forest, several miles east of Lava Butte, is one of the world's largest forests of standing "stone trees." The flow from Lava Butte 6,000 years ago engulfed and buried a pine forest 20 feet deep and quickly drained out. A thin shell of basalt rapidly solidified around the trees, and the wood burned or rotted away, leaving 200 upright cylinders or tubes standing 2 feet above the flow.

NORTH CASCADE MOUNTAINS

The rocks of the North Cascades are a puzzlement. Some of the most ancient sedimentary rocks, more than 50 million years old, have traveled many thousands of miles from their place of origin. The puzzle remains unsolved. The jagged peaks and steep valleys are difficult to explore because of heavy underbrush, glacial ice, and steep terrain.

The North Cascades, unlike the southern Cascades, resulted from crustal uplift and are essentially nonvolcanic. Eight to 10 terranes united far offshore into superterranes, then traveled east on oceanic plates and collided with North America amid a network of faults and a succession of uplift and erosion.

The range has a granite heart with 17 plutons and 8 batholiths uplifted into high peaks. The Golden Horn batholith is one of the West's most massive. Glaciers of at least four ice ages sculpted the sharp, craggy peaks of the North Cascades—"America's Alps." The range boasts nearly 50 waterfalls and 318 glaciers, more than half of the total in the Lower 48, but the glaciers are small now, and all have retreated into the highest mountain basins. Still, glacier melt supplies rivers all summer long.

The highest peak within the park is Mount Shuksan, at 9,131 feet. Glacier Peak is the most remote of Cascade volcanoes, in the midst of Glacier Peak Wilderness. Mount Baker is the most northwesterly peak of the American Cascades. The Pickett Range, which only expert climbers attempt, is a major alpine attraction in the North Cascades.

The North Cascades National Park complex includes the 674,000-acre park, created in 1968, Ross Lake National

North Cascades

The pleasantest winter I ever spent was a summer on Puget Sound," wrote Mark Twain. Someone should have told him that Seattle gets less annual rainfall than any major East Coast city: about 37 inches. Of course, that rain drizzles out over 158 days. Rain, fog, snow—the Pacific Northwest has set national records in all three. In 1931 the most rain recorded in one year in the Lower 48 was 184.56 inches in the community of Wynoochee-Oxbow, located in a rain forest on the southwest flank of Washington's Olympic Mountains. Cape Disappointment, at the mouth of the Columbia River, holds the national record for the most hours of heavy fog a year—2,552. That works out to 106 foggy days each year.

Mount Rainier holds a national record for the most snow falling in one spot during a year: more than 93 feet piled up from February 19, 1971, to February 18, 1972, at Paradise Ranger Station on its southern slope (elevation 5,450 feet). The same area set a national snowfall record for 24 hours— 70 inches from February 23 to 24, 1994. Snowfall is heavier farther up Mount Rainier, but no recording station exists there. At 10,000 feet, snow tapers off because very cold air cannot hold as much moisture. Cold weather on Rainier's upper slopes can rival Mount Everest's: temperatures of minus 55°F, and winds gusting at 100 miles an hour.

The most savage windstorm ever recorded on the West Coast hit the Northwest on Columbus Day in 1962, a typhoon from the Philippines. High winds for 3 to 5 hours along 1,000 miles of the Pacific coast peaked in the Northwest in Washington's Pacific County at 160 miles an hour. Half a million homes were damaged and 47 people died.

A "silver thaw" is glorious to behold, but dangerous. Every few years one of these ice storms, propelled by high winds funneling down from the eastern end of the Columbia Gorge, hits Portland and the western end of the gorge. Roads become too slick to drive on. Trees and power poles pick up increasingly heavy loads of clear ice that can break limbs and fell smaller trees. The ice is caused by relatively warm rain falling on icy surfaces.

Recreation Area (NRA), and Lake Chelan NRA. Stephen Mather Wilderness Area embraces 92 percent of the park and recreation areas. The North Cascades Highway, 100 miles long, runs along the edge of the mountains, and is closed by heavy snow during the winter. One of its imposing outlooks is Washington Pass, 5,477 feet high, with views of spires, pinnacles, and sheer cliffs. (See Batholiths; Glaciers)

OLYMPIC MOUNTAINS

Only a scientist would call mountains 3 million to 12 million years old "young." But the Olympics are among North America's most recently created mountains, and some of their rocks are among the youngest in the world contained in a major mountain range. These peaks are the only ones of the U.S. Coast Ranges to host glaciers, the result of high precipitation and cool summers that don't melt much ice.

When the oceanic plate carrying great deposits of continental sediment began to descend into the ocean trench, some of the lighter sedimentary rock and lava was scraped off onto the continent. A thick layer of the oceanic plate (now called the Crescent Formation) began to rotate slowly, wrapping around the overlying sedimentary rock, forcing a jumble of rock layers to fold, warp, and upend. This coastal slab of oceanic crust may be the thickest ever known. The Crescent Formation, unique in mountain building, stands nearly vertical around much of the Olympic Peninsula.

Ice-age glaciers carved the sandstone peaks, grinding cirques and cutting knife ridges and matterhorns. The new mountains created the Olympic rain shadow, a mountainous wall that forced eastward-bound wet air from the Pacific Ocean to drop its cargo of moisture, 140 to 200 inches of precipitation a year. Rocky peaks form a ragged skyline with deep, steep valleys, craggy peaks, and a multitude of waterfalls.

Because it rises from almost sea level—no peak is more than 30 miles from the sea—the Olympic Range looks higher than it is. Many peaks rise around 4,000 feet; the highest in the entire coastal belt, Mount Olympus, is 7,965 feet. Today 7 of the range's 50 glaciers and icefields grind away at Mount Olympus. The largest is Blue Glacier; the longest is the Hoh (3.8 miles).

The Olympic Peninsula, 60 by 90 miles, is isolated by salt water on three sides. Olympic National Park's nearly roadless, 57-mile-long, undeveloped sea coast is the nation's last undisturbed coastal ecosystem, with one of the nation's longest saltwater shorelines. The Olympic National Marine Sanctuary, the first such sanctuary in the Pacific Northwest, protects 135 nearly roadless miles of shoreline and extends 40 miles out to sea. (See Glaciers; Mountains Cast a Long Shadow)

OREGON COAST

The 362-mile-long Oregon coast has the most varied geological formations—sand dunes, blowholes, tide pools, towering rock monoliths, marshes and bogs, a natural sea cave—of any coast anywhere of similar size. It also reveals one of the most unspoiled and least developed coastlines on the U.S. mainland. Recreation areas or state parks every 5 miles form one of the nation's best such networks.

Nearly a dozen capes and headlands rise impressively, often projecting far out into the ocean. Many were formed of Columbia Plateau flood basalts. Cape Foulweather offers a museum of different lava types. Formerly an offshore volcanic island, the cape uplifted at the same time as Heceta Head, Oregon's Coast Range, and Cape Perpetua, highest point on the Oregon coast.

Tillamook Head, one of Oregon's largest coastal monoliths at 1,136 feet, comprises a complex assemblage of eroded headlands, coves, sea stacks, arches, and Tillamook Rock, an offshore basaltic sea stack 100 feet high. Cape Lookout, 700 feet high, may have once been an offshore volcanic island. Cape

Kiwanda, formed of uplifted sandstone, is protected from the surf by a large basaltic sea "haystack" just offshore. Windy Cape Blanco, Oregon's westernmost point, is known for its white mollusk fossils. Near Cape Arago, offshore stacks are remnants of sandstone that once formed a continuous headland.

Protection of the beaches, natural landmarks, and wildlife began in 1907 with Three Arch Rocks near Tillamook. In 1913 all Oregon beaches were declared public highways, since they were used as roads during low tides where forests were too thick and headlands or hillsides too steep and rocky for road building. Not until 1936 was the winding coastal highway built. In the late 1960s, new laws protected Otter Rock, Haystack Rock, and Cape Perpetua. In 1982 the Oregon Islands National Wildlife Refuge was created, including most of the 1,400 islands, offshore rocks, and reefs. The Oregon Beach Law of 1967 proclaimed the right of "free and uninterrupted use" of beaches by the public, from the Columbia River to the California border, right up to the line of vegetation, with access at least every 3 miles.

Oregon Coast

This recreational easement also preserved tide pools, offshore rocks, dunes, estuaries, and coastal forests. (See Dunes; Caves; Time and Tide Pools)

PALOUSE HILLS

Did Coyote really scoop the Palouse soil into those undulating hills so that he could win a race with Turtle from the Snake River to Spokane County? The truth is that the wind did it. Wind-borne loess of the richly productive Palouse Hills in eastern Washington and Idaho rates among the most fertile of all Northwest soil. Covering an area 85 by 100 miles and straddling the Idaho–Washington border, that soil produces crops of wheat, peas, and lentils of greater quantity and of superior quality to those grown in most other regions of North America.

The soil—soft, fine-textured, yellowish brown—derives from silt blowing for thousands of years into the Palouse on the prevailing northeasterly winds from the White Bluffs near Hanford and from glacial outwash deposits, old dunes, and ancient lakebeds of the Pasco Basin. It may have begun as glacial "rock flour." Ash eruptions from Glacier Peak, Mount Mazama, and Mount St. Helens added volume and minerals.

Deposits of loess are thickest and most continuous in the eastern part of Washington's rolling Palouse Hills. Thinner layers of the soil cover much of the Pasco Basin and northern Oregon. Thin layers are also found from Pendleton to The Dalles. In Idaho only a few mounded hills of loess are left near Moscow and Pocatello, perhaps because Idaho's active mountain streams have stripped off soil.

The Palouse Hills are really dunes, with the steeper part facing the direction in which they are moving. Randomly arranged, they lack normal drainage networks. The soil is highly vulnerable to erosion—by wind and water runoff. Even with improved farming methods, the water in the Palouse River and Palouse Falls (185 feet high) often runs brown and thick with silt in the spring. (See Missoula Floods)

RIVERS

The Cascade Mountains divide the Pacific Northwest's drainage systems, with westside rivers flowing into salt water and eastside rivers flowing into the Columbia. Even Idaho's rivers, all but one, drain into the mighty Columbia.

Washington's 14 major rivers and 10 minor rivers on the west side of the Cascades and Olympics empty into either Puget Sound or the Pacific Ocean. Westside rivers draining much of the North Cascades include the Skagit (Washington's most powerful river after the Columbia), Stillaguamish,

Nooksack, and Snohomish; rivers flowing east of the North Cascades include the Wenatchee, Methow, and Stehekin. From the central Cascades, westside rivers include the Chehalis, Puyallup, and Nisqually. In the Olympic Mountains, rivers draining to the west include the Hoh, Quinault, Queets, and Quillayute; on the east are the Hamma Hamma, Duckabush, Dosewallips, and Quilcene.

Oregon's drainage includes more than a dozen smaller rivers on the west side of the Coast Range that empty directly into the sea. Some of Oregon's rivers, including the Deschutes and John Day, run north to the Columbia. Oregon's largest river is the Willamette, recently named one of 14 Heritage Rivers in the United States. It collects drainage from the west side of Oregon's southern Cascades and

> Oregon's largest river is the Willamette, recently named one of the 14 Heritage Rivers in the United States.
> •

from the east side of the Coast Range, emptying into the Columbia. More than four dozen of Oregon's many rivers, with their narrow, steep-sided canyons, have been designated Wild and Scenic, such as the Illinois and Owyhee. The Rogue, one of the few rivers powerful enough to cut through rising mountains to the Pacific, originates in springs northwest of Crater Lake. The Rogue cut a canyon 2,000 feet deep and in its 215-mile rush to the sea drops 5,300 feet.

All of Idaho's rivers—including the Salmon, Clearwater, Lochsa, Selway, Clark Fork, and St. Joe—eventually feed into the Columbia, except for the Bear River, which ends up in Utah's Great Salt Lake. Idaho has more than a half dozen Wild and Scenic–designated rivers. The 425-mile-long Salmon River, second largest in Idaho, earns its nickname, River of No Return, with more than 40 rapids. The nation's longest free-flowing river was only partially mapped as

late as 1949. The Salmon has carved two of the nation's three deepest gorges: Salmon Canyon on the Main Salmon and Impossible Canyon on the Middle Fork. (See Messages From the Underground; Columbia River)

SPRINGS

Some like 'em hot, some like 'em cold. Most Pacific Northwest springs emerge in Oregon and Idaho. Springwater originates either as rain or as "juvenile water" (water from deep inside the earth that reaches the surface for the first time). Mineral hot springs hold dissolved minerals such as sulfur, sodium chloride, and magnesium sulfate, and gases such as hydrogen sulfide and carbon dioxide that fizz up the water.

Idaho's Big Spring, ranked among the nation's 40 largest cold springs, discharges 120 million gallons of water a day, providing the headwaters for Henrys Fork River. Early travelers in Idaho raved about Thousand Springs, where hundreds of aquifer-fed springs gushed from the bare rock cliffs of the Snake River Canyon near Hagerman. But many of the springs were diverted long ago for irrigation and fish farming. Today only a few cascade out.

At Lava Hot Springs, south of Pocatello, more than 100 steaming springs pour out 6.7 million gallons a day.

•

River aquifer, reappearing miles away as hot and cold springs. One of Idaho's hottest (178°F) issues at Bonneville campground. Lehman Hot Springs in the Wallowa-Whitman National Forest, one of the Northwest's largest, was once a gathering place for the Nez Perce.

In the basin and range country of Oregon and Idaho, many thermal springs occur along valley margins or from faults at the edge of much-fractured batholiths. Oregon possesses prime geological conditions for hot springs: extensive faulting; snowmelt and rainfall; cracked, broken, and jointed rock. Nearly 100 thermal springs vary from 70°F to 198°F (Breitenbush and Vale). Dozens of thermal springs cluster in southeastern and southcentral Oregon.

Many of southern Idaho's hot springs originate in its huge Snake

At Lava Hot Springs, south of Pocatello, more than 100 steaming, highly mineralized springs issue from vents along a creek at the base of high lava cliffs, pouring out 6.7 million gallons a day, 1,500 gallons a minute. The spring-fed pools stay between 104°F and 110°F. (See Messages From the Underground; In Hot Water)

WATERFALLS

They bedazzle the senses—beauty in perpetual motion, thundering like a distant ocean. The three Northwest states boast the largest, most varied, and most accessible assortment of waterfalls in the United States—more than 500 of them in different styles: plunge, horsetail, block, fan, tier, punch bowl.

Shoshone Falls

North America's densest group of falls plunge over bare basalt cliffs along Oregon's Columbia River Gorge National Scenic Area. Some 77 falls tumble along the south side of the gorge, with most falls within 20 miles of each other; 11 catapult down more than 100 feet. The Road of Falling Waters passes 9 major falls within 10 miles, including two-tiered Multnomah Falls, fourth-highest year-round falls in the nation at 620 feet.

Within or near Washington's Mount Rainier National Park, 123 major waterfalls plunge over rocky ledges. Two of the largest, Clear Creek and Sluiskin Falls, cascade 300 feet. Comet Falls—the result of glaciation, as are most of Mount Rainier's waterfalls—plunges 320 feet from a hanging valley.

Idaho's pride, Shoshone Falls, on the Snake River 5 miles east of Twin Falls, is the Northwest's largest cataract, 1,000 to 1,500 feet wide—depending on how much irrigation water is being diverted. The broad waterfall thunders down 212 feet over massive, horseshoe-shaped ledges. Twin Falls was created in the same way. (See Missoula Floods)

BATHOLITHS

Pushy. Intrusive. Meet the batholith, a granitic mass that solidified often miles beneath the earth's surface. The hot magma stretched and pushed rocks apart, deformed country rock to make space for its plumes, pried out blocks, and injected itself into dikes, sills, and fractures. The emplacement of Pacific Northwest batholiths and plutons occurred during the climactic, final phase of mountain building.

The Idaho Batholith ranks as the Northwest's most extensive granite mass. Some 200 miles long, north to south, and 75 miles wide, the batholith comprises two separate but neighboring batholiths. The Bitterroot section to the north, and the larger

Atlanta to the south, cover 15,400 square miles in central and western Idaho and up into the Panhandle. Emplaced 7 to 10 miles under the surface perhaps 70 million years ago, the Idaho Batholith was uplifted as a crystalline core into Idaho's high, jagged mountains. It underlies half of the glacier-sculpted Sawtooth Range, along with the smaller, younger Sawtooth Batholith.

The movement through the earth of the Bitterroot section of Idaho's batholith destabilized overlying sedimentary layers that arched and folded. Layers of ancient sedimentary rock 10 miles thick cracked off and traveled 50 miles east in a million years, forming two mountain ranges in western Montana. With the

Sawtooth Mountains

weight of 10 miles of rock removed, the ground that contained the batholith was uplifted the same distance, to become the core of Idaho's high mountains. Several rivers—the Snake, Salmon, Lochsa, and Selway—have cut deep canyons into the granite.

A similar process formed batholiths or plutons in other high mountains of the Northwest, especially in the North Cascades and under Mount Rainier. (Tatoosh Pluton, only 1½ miles deep, intrudes Mount Rainier and also forms the sharp pinnacles of Tatoosh Ridge.)

Underlying much of the central North Cascades, the Snoqualmie Batholith (25 to 17 million years young) formed only 1½ miles deep. Washington's Mount Stuart, the state's oldest pluton at 88 million years, was a "stitching" pluton that injected magma into fault zones at the continent's edge, securing the new accretions.

Oregon's largest pluton, the Wallowa Batholith, forms the core of the Blue and Wallowa Mountains, uplifted after the accretion of five separate terranes, which united near the Idaho Batholith. (See In Hot Water; Gem Minerals; Gold)

COLUMBIA PLATEAU FLOOD BASALT

Seldom has lava flowed in such volume, covered so extensive an area (200,000 square miles), or recurred with such long intervals between flows (tens of thousands of years). The Columbia Plateau, one of the world's largest volcanic provinces, encompasses most of eastern Washington and Oregon, and much of Idaho's western edge. Although commonly called a plateau, it is really a giant basin.

Among the five major flows, the Grande Ronde was responsible for more than 85 percent of the lava. Later flows thinly covered much of the Grande Ronde lava, which flowed perhaps every 10,000 years between 16.5 million and 14.5 million years ago. The largest lava flow was the Roza member of the Grande Ronde, more than 300 miles long. The 15-million-year-old flow can be traced from Grand Coulee east to Spokane, south to Pendleton, and southwest into the Columbia River Gorge. It stopped just short of the ocean.

More than 4,800 square miles of mountainous terrain in western Idaho were filled in and the drainage of the Snake River was forced to move to the southwest. Quietly the magma welled up, often from tens of thousands of fissures fed by the same reservoir. When a flow ceased, the magma remaining in fractures and in the surface fissures solidified. Many fissures stretched more than 25 feet across and were tens of miles long, trending north and northwest.

A typical flow could pile up 100 feet high, allowing the shrinkage columns (columnar jointing) to form impressive colonnades up to a mile long. Polygonal cracks formed in the cooling lava as it crystallized down from the top and up from the bottom. The two never met exactly, so there is always a jumbled meeting place of rubble—the entablature. The thin lava tended to pond several hundred feet thick in eastern and central Washington basins, such as Pasco and Yakima. Each flow, moving perhaps 25 miles an hour downhill, could last several hours to several days.

Originally, the Columbia River flowed to the ocean much farther south in Oregon, perhaps emptying at Tillamook. When the new coastal range in Oregon abruptly migrated 50 miles to the north, it pushed the river estuary along with it. Some Grande Ronde lava flowed down antecedent channels of the Columbia River. Each time its channel was plugged hundreds of feet deep with lava, the Columbia cut a new channel to the north, always maintaining its course to the Pacific. Those ocean-bound lavas spilled over into the Willamette Valley as far south as Salem. One notable flow near Hood River poured into the Columbia River Gorge from both sides, forming a temporary shore-to-shore bridge: the Native Americans' Bridge of the Gods, perhaps.

The maximum depth of the lava is unknown. A well drilled 6,000 feet deep near Yakima failed to pass through the basalt flows. The thick flows have hidden many clues to the Northwest's geological history.

EARTHQUAKES

The greatest danger of high-magnitude, long-duration earthquakes in the Northwest lies in shallow coastal regions close to an active subduction zone, such as the 600-mile-long Cascadia Subduction Zone 50 miles offshore. There, the heavier oceanic plate heads eastward into a subduction trench, for recycling 60 miles down, usually going gently. But occasionally it snags, bulging up the overriding North American plate. Pressure builds up for years until the upper plate suddenly drops—a quake.

A magnitude 9.0 earthquake with a rapid drop of 2 to 8 feet can cause a tidal wave or tsunami. Evidence along the Oregon and Washington coast suggests a number of tsunamis have occurred over the past few thousand years. In the spring of 1998 a 2,000-year-old forest of 200 Sitka spruce and western red cedar stumps was slowly exposed on an Oregon beach near Neskowin. The stumps suggested that a powerful earthquake had suddenly dropped the coast 7 feet killing trees with salt water, and burying them deeply with a massive sand shift.

Western Washington has endured 33 major quakes in the past 12,000 years. The most severe earthquake in Washington's recorded history, magnitude 7.0, shook the southern Puget Sound area in April 1949 and was felt over 150,000 square miles.

In October 1983 a mammoth quake, magnitude 7.1 and 9 miles deep, hit Idaho's Thousand Springs Valley along a fault zone on the south flank of Lost River Range, fault-block mountains in

> **Evidence along the Oregon and Washington coast suggests a number of tsunamis have occurred over the past few thousand years.**
>
> ●

the basin and range province. Over the next 48 hours, the Snake River Plain Aquifer spewed 400 billion gallons of water 10 to 20 feet into the air. Liquefaction of water-saturated sand and silt created quicksand-like surfaces. More than 40 blowhole craters formed. Old Faithful, some 300 miles away, lengthened its interval between eruptions by 8 minutes. Within 15 seconds, Lost River Fault, which runs for 10,000 feet, suddenly opened up for 25 miles. Aftershocks continued for 10 months. Frequent earthquakes along the edges of the basin and range province indicate the faults are still active.

FOSSILS

In Clarkia Lake in Idaho's Panhandle, 1 cubic foot of sedimentary rock yielded

1,000 separate plant fossils of many genera and species. In 1990 an unusual magnolia leaf was found at Clarkia. Although 17 million years old, it was still green and contained undamaged strands of DNA, the oldest ever found undamaged.

In the Latah Formation, which straddles Idaho's border with Washington, beautifully preserved leaves have been found, especially of deciduous trees, including ginkgo, plum, fig, poplar, magnolia, maple, bald cypress, and metasequoia. Siltstones in Washington's Bellingham Bay yield palm frond fossil imprints 3 feet across.

Other fossilized palm fronds have turned up in Cottage Grove, Oregon, and in the rich Eagle Creek flora of the Columbia Gorge.

In the Okanogan Highlands, near the town of Republic, the

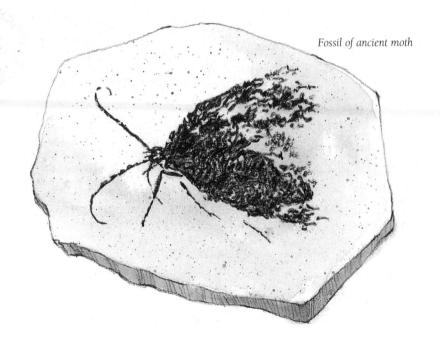

Fossil of ancient moth

vegetation preserved was of the upland variety—roses instead of palms. An upland conifer forest there contained species of pine and the earliest macroscopic records of hemlock, spruce, red cedar, and fir. Nearly a dozen fruits familiar today left their oldest fossil records near Republic at least 15 to 17 million years ago, including apple, blackberry, grape, pear, cherry, and red raspberry. Parts of insects such as earwig pincers have been found, and a rare imprint of an entire moth.

In Idaho's Hagerman Valley near Thousand Springs, the Hagerman fauna site runs for several miles in a river bluff on the west side of Snake River Canyon, the world's most important Pliocene site, 5 million to 7 million years old. Fossils in the area, now a national natural landmark, include camel, giant bison, musk ox, giant ground sloth, giant beaver, and the inevitable predators: cougarlike cats, weasels, badgers, coyotes, and a scavenger dog.

Eastern Washington's Blue Lake Rhinoceros Cave is the only mammal mold ever found within a lava flow. An aquatic species of rhinoceros, *diceratherium*, weighing about a ton, was floating upside-down in a shallow pond, legs stiffened in death. Lava flowed into the water and formed pillow basalt—baglike formations with a tough outer skin and flexible insides—all around the rhino. Their protection prevented the weight of subsequent lava flows from shattering the bones. Then about 12,000 years ago, the Missoula floods gouged away lava in the canyon's west wall where the rhino mold was concealed. The floodwaters created an opening just large enough—2 feet by 1½ feet—for a man to squeeze through. In 1935 one did, and discovered that the cave was really an animal mold, with four dark holes in the roof marking the legs and a larger hole in the floor marking the head. Some rhinoceros bones lying within the mold included a toothless right jaw and a lower left jaw with a complete second molar. (See John Day Fossil Beds)

GREAT RIFT

One of the largest, best-exposed major rift systems in the Lower 48, the Great Rift of the Snake River plain curves from Idaho's Pioneer Mountains to the Sublett Mountain Range. The rift, a complex zone of parallel faults and fissures, has stretched and weakened the earth's crust. More than two dozen cinder cones and some 60 north-south flows issued from it. Eight eruptive periods occurred, beginning 15,000 years ago and ending only 2,100 years ago. The first featured 2-mile-long lava fountains of molten, gas-charged rock that formed symmetrical cones as it cooled. The final stage ended with viscous lava forming spatter cones.

At least three separate lava fields, in addition to Craters of the Moon along the rift's northern edge, form part of the Great Rift National Monument. The green-blue, iridescent Blue Dragon flow of lava surrounding Craters of the Moon makes up most of the rift surface. Hells Half Acre volcanic field, over 2 miles long, is second in size to Craters of the Moon. King's Bowl, located directly over a Great Rift fracture, is a huge crater 280 feet long and 1,000 feet deep. Crystal Ice Cave passes through it, formed by surface water that penetrated a lava tube cave and froze. (See Craters of the Moon)

JOHN DAY FOSSIL BEDS

Around 50 million to 5 million years ago, elephants, saber-toothed cats, rhinos, tapirs, and tiny horses roamed the now-arid Oregon basin of John Day Fossil Beds. They left proof in bone fragments preserved in layers of volcanic ash up to 1,000 feet deep, topped by Columbia Plateau flood basalts. John Day Fossil Beds National Monument contains fossils of more than 120 animal species. On Sheep Rock, a horn-tipped promontory 3,360 feet high, capped with lava, 40 million years of the basin's geological history can be read.

The Clarno Formation is one of the few places in the world where fossilized plant leaves, stems, seeds, and nuts are all found together. Plants ranged from tropical species—avocado, magnolia, and fig—to deciduous species—oak and hickory—better adapted to the cooler weather that followed. The many mudflows and rock slides impounded lushly forested ponds, which accumulated animal and plant remains and the fine-grained sediment to entomb them. The debris later eroded into bronze-colored, badlands pinnacles and palisades.

The John Day Formation contains the richest concentration of prehistoric mammalian fossils in the nation—the longest nearly

Sheep Rock at John Day Fossil Beds

• VOLCANOES ANCIENT AND MODERN •

Mount St. Helens, post-eruption

Imagine an eruption 42 times more powerful than Mount St. Helens' blowup in 1980. Ancient Mount Mazama blew itself apart 7,700 years ago and left as its legacy Crater Lake. This volcano, highest of the southern Cascade Range, may have been Oregon's highest, at 12,000 feet. Built on a base of older basalt shield volcanoes, it was a complex of low domes and stratocones. The volcano was active off and on for perhaps half a million years, with long periods of quiet punctuated by violent pumice and ash eruptions.

During its last eruption, it spewed out the largest amount of pumice and ash known to have been ejected by a recent Cascade volcano. Ash filled nearby canyons 250 feet deep. The finest ash reached central Montana and Saskatchewan. Glowing avalanches of pumice frothed down the mountain at 100 miles an hour. Some flows carried pumice boulders up to 114 feet in diameter for 20 miles. A glowing avalanche swept across Diamond Lake, leaving behind pumice piles 30 feet thick.

Blanketing 350,000 square miles in Washington, Oregon, and Idaho with 42 cubic miles of pyroclastic material, Mount Mazama must have erupted for several days. Scientists used the notorious Mazama ash, easily identified by its yellowish tint, for dating other events in Northwest geologic history.

With the magma chamber empty, the undermined summit collapsed, reducing Mount Mazama by 2,500 feet. A later lava flow produced a cinder cone (now named Wizard Island) that displays Mazama's youngest rocks Phantom Ship, a 161-foot-high lava dike visible in Crater Lake, may hold ➤

• VOLCANOES ANCIENT AND MODERN *cont.* •

the oldest rocks in Crater Lake National Park—400,000 years old. Filling the caldera with water from rain and snowmelt could have taken 700 to 1,500 years.

The 1980 eruption of Mount St. Helens in Washington was one of the first major volcanic eruptions to be extensively monitored. Ten new seismographs installed just two months before, registered 1,000 deep earthquakes before the main event. On May 18 an earthquake of magnitude 5.1 triggered a slide on the volcano's bulging north slope. An explosion of highly pressurized, superheated gases hurled out 3 billion to 4 billion cubic yards of rock debris, glacial ice, and ash. Traveling 70 to 150 miles an hour, it buried the valley of the North Fork of the Toutle River 50 to 600 feet deep and dumped 0.6 cubic mile of debris over 25 square miles.

An unexpected fan-shaped lateral blast of superhot (570°F) gas, rocks, ash, and steam quickly overtook the avalanche, accelerating from 220 to 670 miles an hour—the speed of sound. The blast killed animals and plants up to 23 miles away, pulverizing, incinerating, leveling 150,000 acres of forest 19 miles away. Within 10 minutes of the eruption, a vertical plume with a purple cauliflower-shaped cloud edged with lightning spewed out for 9 hours 540 million tons of ash and pumice at least 12 miles into the air. The ash drifted down on 22,000 square miles, circling the earth during the next two weeks.

Several hours after the eruption, a lahar picked up everything in its path—trees, boulders, houses—scouring soil down to bedrock at speeds of up to 250 miles an hour for 50 miles. The mudflow dumped 100 million cubic yards of sediment into the lower reaches of the Cowlitz River and the Columbia River. Navigation channels in the Columbia were clogged for nearly 3 months.

There were surprises: the rock-carrying "stone wind" that stripped trees of bark; the powerful lateral blast; the many animal and plant survivors protected in burrows, under the ice of ponds, within wood, behind mounds and rocks. Ants were soon active; spiders parachuted in. Elk quickly returned in large numbers to browse shrubs and newly planted trees. Their droppings fertilized the ash and their hoofs left prints in the ash where wind-carried seeds germinated. Pocket gophers protected in the ground quickly pushed rich soil up on top of the ash, in which seeds sprouted. A heavy rainfall that year also helped wash the ash away. (See Cascade Volcanoes)

continuous record found anywhere. Ash—sometimes incandescent flows—inundated the landscape, smothering and burying animals. The aridity helped preserve the fossils, as did the many layers of basalt lava, as deep as 30 feet.

John Day and Clarno Formations display some of the nation's most colorful volcanic ash: rust red, pale green, yellow, creamy buff. The gently rounded hills of the Painted Hills unit are especially delicate in color. Also eye-catching are the extensive, 7-million-year-old, brick red ridges of welded tuff, formed when particles of volcanic debris fused from the heat. Thousands of thunder eggs have been found among those hard ridges.

New finds continue to be made: a fossilized walnut, a small piece of banana 43 million years old, a molar from a 5-pound lemurlike primate 25 million years old, a 7-million-year-old claw sheath of a saber-toothed cat, fossilized bones from two new species of bear-dogs, and three types of extinct elephants. Buried treasure remains! (See Agates; Thunder Eggs; Fossils)

MISSOULA FLOODS

Water, water everywhere. About 15,000 years ago Glacial Lake Missoula, the largest known ice-dammed lake in the world, backed up in Clark Fork River Canyon behind a lobe of continental ice. After filling tributary valleys for 30 to 70 years, the lake was 150 miles long and high enough to topple the ice dam. A wall of water 2,000 feet high rushed out of the mile-wide canyon mouth at 45 to 60 miles an hour. Heading southwest with the tilt of the land, the floodwaters passed through Lakes Coeur d'Alene and Pend Oreille, and into the Spokane and Little Spokane Rivers.

On the Columbia Plateau, the waters divided into several streams. One ravaged the Channeled

Scablands, stripping off several hundred feet of fertile soil and chewing up the basalt bedrock. Another stream rushed through nearly a dozen coulees, deepening them, scooping out caves, and tearing chunks from the walls.

> **Dry Falls, linking Upper and Lower Grand Coulees, was once the world's largest waterfall.**
>
> ●

Even the mighty Columbia, larger then, could not break its ice dam, but it overflowed onto the plateau, mixing with the floodwaters. Dry Falls, once the world's largest waterfall, linked Upper and Lower Grand Coulees; it testifies to the power of the flood. The crest of the several deeply notched, horseshoe-shaped cliffs runs for 3½ miles with a fall of 400 feet.

The various streams merged temporarily at the southern end of Lower Grand Coulee in broad Quincy Basin, where they dropped tons of sand and gravel before rushing on to Wallula Gap, the only passage through the Cascades, cut earlier by the Columbia River. Along the way, the floodwaters stranded many icebergs containing boulders rafted in from Montana.

All the waters ended up behind the gap, forming temporary Lake Lewis—1,000 feet deep and covering 3,000 square miles of Pasco Basin.

Gradually the iceberg-cluttered floodwaters passed through Wallula Gap, only to back up again at The Dalles in temporary Lake Condon. The water was heading for the ocean now, scouring the gorge walls and abandoning icebergs on ledges.

One last lake formed, Lake Allison, in the Willamette Valley near the bend in the Columbia River near Portland. Erratics dropped from stranded icebergs around the lakeshores indicate a water depth of 400 feet. At last that lake drained, and the flood was soon over. It may have lasted only a week.

Many more floods were to follow, but this was probably the largest and most catastrophic. The Ice Age was waning and later ice dams were lower, holding less water behind them. (See Grand Coulee; Erratics)

• IN HOT WATER •

The town of Klamath Falls in southwest Oregon is perpetually in hot water. Most of the city lies atop a subterranean geothermal reservoir, one of the most extensive underlying any city in the western hemisphere—2 miles wide, 6.8 miles long. Scarps rise on either side of the city, which is located in a trough that was dropped along a fault. Hot rock lies at a shallow depth beneath Klamath Falls, and the ancient lake beds that underlie most of the Klamath Lake lowlands form a watertight lid over the hot rocks, trapping the naturally heated water.

Most hot springs produce water heated as it circulates along deep fractures in the earth's crust. Native Americans and early settlers bathed in and cooked with water from the many hot springs that once flowed in Klamath Falls. But 500 wells—public and private—diverted the water and dried up the springs. Because the mineralized water, like most naturally heated water, clogs and corrodes pipes, down-hole heat exchangers are used to heat normal ground water, which then flows into buildings. The resource is protected by cascading successive uses of the water from hottest to coolest, and reinjecting the cooled water into the aquifer through special wells.

Boise, Idaho, also sits atop a large, naturally occurring geothermal reservoir. Imbedded layers of clay, basalt, sand, and gravel, underlie the Boise Front Geothermal Aquifer in a zone of faults and fractures 3,030 feet deep. Hot water at 160°F to 170° F, trapped by porous sandstone and deeply fractured volcanic rocks more than 1,000 feet deep, rises to within a few hundred feet of the surface. Geothermal water flows slowly along the fault, concentrating along the north margin of the Snake River Plain downwarp.

As in Klamath Falls, wells have dried up naturally occurring springs. Most government buildings in Boise are geothermally heated. Although hot springs are plentiful in both Idaho and Oregon, the supply of this non-polluting heat source is usually far removed from the area of demand, and it doesn't travel well.

AGATES AND THUNDER EGGS

They're Cinderella stones, those thunder eggs (geodes). Ranging from a fraction of an inch to grapefruit size, geodes have a brown, knobby, ridged rind of an exterior, but when you saw them in half, it's fairy-godmother time. The handsome interior may be star shaped, full of quartz crystals or banded in several colors of agate. No two thunder eggs are exactly alike.

Agates, essentially quartz, can form in the cavities and

veins of any rock, but the Northwest's abundant silica-rich lava, with its many gas cavities, provides the ideal matrix. Groundwater circulating through the lava very slowly precipitates out silica minerals—quartz, opal, chalcedony (a translucent blue or gray quartz)—that eventually fill the cavities over many thousands of years. More thousands of years

Thunder Egg

may pass before the filled nodules erode out of the ash beds.

The Northwest states lead the nation in amount and variety of agates and thunder eggs. Agate pebbles are scattered along ocean beaches in southern Oregon, where winter storms constantly unearth new ones, and in stream or gravel riverbeds in Idaho, often on hillside terraces above streams. In gemstone-rich Idaho, agates with plumes of white, red, yellow, and blue are found in veins a foot wide at Graveyard Point and in hillside terraces above streams. The state also yields moss agates, agates with branched designs like trees (dendritic) or threads (rutilated), agates with landscapes (picture agates), blue agates, and banded agates (including onyx). Agate hunters uncover scarce Ellensburg blue agates in eastern Washington's Teanaway Ridge and in the Ellensburg Formation. Washington's North Cascades contain banded, moss, and plume agates.

Most of the nations' thunder eggs—Oregon's official state rock—are found in arid central and southeastern Oregon, north of Bend in such places as the Ochoco Mountains, Madras, and Prineville; Steens and Hart Mountains; and, by the thousands, in ledges of welded ash (6-million-year-old volcanic rock called tuff) in the John Day Fossil Beds.

ERRATICS

Orphans among Northwest rocks, erratics were abandoned far from home. Such rocks, from pebbles to boulders, are found in regions where they do not naturally occur. Most granite, quartzite, gneiss, and slate found in Oregon originated in Idaho or Montana. These rocks lie scattered by the hundreds over the Columbia Plateau from Grand Coulee down to Pasco Basin, left on ledges in the Columbia Gorge and on Sauvie Island in the Columbia River. Largest and most dramatic are erratics shaped like huge haystacks that loom up in farmers' fields in northeastern Washington. The huge blocks of black basalt were plucked from the northern rim of the Columbia Plateau by the Canadian ice sheet, which extended as far south as Lake Chelan. Many haystack rocks ended up near Withrow Moraine at the mouth of Moses Coulee, where the ice made its last stand before melting back. Some erratics were left nearly 5,000 feet high on the Twin Sisters Peaks near Mount Baker.

In Pasco Basin and the Willamette Valley, the erratics show up more than 100 miles south of the margins of continental ice, obviously rafted in by floodwater icebergs. Hundreds were stranded in Lake Allison, a temporary body of water 400 feet deep that filled much of the Willamette Valley during the Missoula floods. Erratic Rock State Park near McMinnville was created around a single huge slate erratic.

The most "out-of-this-world" erratic ever found in the United States may have been the Willamette Meteorite discovered in the Willamette Valley in 1902. Cone-shaped and partly embedded, it weighed more than 13 tons—the largest ever found in the United States. It was long thought to have fallen at the spot where it was found; many geologists now believe it was rafted in on icebergs from Montana during the Missoula floods. Like other erratics, it was found 400 feet up from the valley floor. Local Indians dubbed it "the visitor from the moon." Before a battle, they dipped arrowheads into rainwater that filled surface pits on the meteorite. (See Missoula Floods)

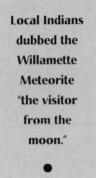

Local Indians dubbed the Willamette Meteorite "the visitor from the moon."

GEM MINERALS

A gem of a state, Idaho. Almost every county offers at least one gem mineral or opalized and agatized wood and fossils. A mineral of gemstone quality is most likely to be found in river terraces, placer deposits, old mining dumps, and gravelly streambeds. Idaho's super-abundance of gem minerals results from plutonic intrusions, glacial erosion, uplifting of mountains, and thousands of square miles of silica-rich rhyolite lava and granite on the Snake River plain.

Crystals such as red garnet, black tourmaline, golden topaz, smoky quartz, and beryls can grow inside pegmatites, often found in ancient rocks near Idaho's great batholiths. A pegmatite is coarse-grained igneous rock with a central gas cavity lined with crystals varying from several inches to many feet. Crystals grow large because pegmatites cool slowly. One at Idaho's City of Rocks measures 300 feet along its smallest dimension.

Garnets, the most widely distributed gem mineral in Idaho, are found in various rock types and colors, including lime green at

Quartz

the Seven Devils complex. Idaho is one of only two places in the world where star garnets, the state's official gemstone, are found. The star results from fiberlike mineral impurities finer than hair. Latah County is world famous for its almandite garnets (ruby red or purplish), some with precious four- or six-rayed stars. A 2-pound garnet was sluiced out of Emerald Creek in northern Idaho in 1983.

In North America only Idaho continues to mine opals commercially. Fire opals discovered in Idaho at the turn of the century equaled in prismatic color (red, yellow, blue, green) any opals in the world. In Idaho's Palouse Hills, precious opals were sometimes found in the late 1800s when wells were dug.

Idaho's Adams County has yielded a few flawless, gem-quality beryl stones (emerald, aquamarine, golden beryl). The heavy stones concentrate in pockets. Beryl is too brittle to withstand tumbling in gravel.

Bear Lake County, Idaho, yields red jasper spiked with green malachite needles. Grass green malachite appears as incrustations in copper mines. Boise County tourmaline crystals sometimes are pink at one end and green at the other.

Most of Washington's gem minerals, although not abundant, occur in the north, associated with North Cascades plutons. Amethysts of good color are found in Walker Valley, southeast of Mount Vernon. Fire opals occasionally turn up near Pullman. Washington's other gem minerals include jasper, well-colored garnets, jadeite, tourmaline, beryl, and malachite.

Oregon takes pride in its state gem, sunstone, as well as jasper, bloodstone, pink rhodonite, and fire opals. Serpentine rock in the Klamath Mountains sometimes offers striking aggregates of red garnets and green jadeite. Some central coastal beaches yield jadeite pebbles. (See Batholiths, Petrified Wood)

GOLD

The prospectors who rushed to the Pacific Northwest in the mid-1800s were following an ancient impulse. Gold has been washed out of rivers or river sands since at least 1200 B.C. Sheepskins—the golden fleece—were once used to collect gold. Common in the earth's crust in small amounts, gold is rarely found in large concentrations. Most precious metals in the

• ALL THAT GLITTERS •

Have gold pan, will travel." Rumors of gold strikes in the 1850s and 1860s in the Pacific Northwest attracted thousands of would-be millionaires, including many who hadn't made it in California. Placer mining in river gravels required a minimum of equipment and expertise. Knowledgeable prospectors looked for sandbars in swift streams and always checked the inner curve or river bend, where rivers lose speed because of widening or curving. Placer mining skimmed the easy gold—grains and nuggets in addition to gold dust. One gold nugget found in Baker County weighed 80.4 ounces.

Gold was first discovered in Oregon in 1851 in Josephine Creek on the Illinois River. The next year Jacksonville became the first boomtown of the Northwest, richest of the Siskiyou mining camps. Canyon Creek brought thousands of miners and yielded millions of dollars. For a few years the easiest placer gold came from Gold Beach on the Oregon coast, at the mouth of the Rogue River. The sandy beaches and river terraces glittered with gold, but a flood in 1861 washed most of the deposits out to sea.

Rivers like the John Day, which drains the western side of the gold-rich Blue Mountains, left gold in local streams—$30 million worth at Whisky Flat. The Cornucopia mines yielded $16 million in gold over 60 years. Once the easy placer gold was removed, the machines moved in for the hard-rock mining that continued for years in some places: blasting, drilling, crushing. The Blue Mountains and Klamath-Siskiyous were especially productive. ➤

Northwest are closely associated with great masses of granite—batholiths that formed the core of most Pacific Northwest mountain ranges.

The precious ores are usually found not within the granitic intrusions but along their margins, where host rocks have been deformed and often shattered. Lode gold was often discovered high in the mountains, because, during mountain building, batholiths or smaller plutons were uplifted along with "host" rocks.

• ALL THAT GLITTERS *cont.* •

Idaho, only a place to pass through quickly during Oregon Trail days, suddenly became a destination after gold was discovered. In 1860 gold was found in Idaho's Orofino Creek. In 1866 Leesburg, on the Salmon River, provided the richest placering grounds in mining history, with $40 million in coarse gold and nuggets. In Idaho's Yankee Fork in 1875 gold ore found in a bedrock vein exposed by erosion was so rich that the unrefined ore was shipped to Salt Lake City for treatment, yielding $5 million of gold and silver. One-fourth of all Idaho gold was taken from placer concentrations. From 1862 to 1869, placer mining around Idaho City was so productive that the town became the largest in the Northwest. More gold was mined near it than in all of Alaska.

In 1884 a bonanza of silver, lead, and zinc was found in Panhandle lake country, where placer gold mining had begun in 1881. The Coeur d'Alene mining district, a 20-mile area within the canyon of the South Fork of the Coeur d'Alene River, became one of the world's richest mining areas. Gold soon became a by-product of silver mining. More silver and lead came out of the ground there from 1886 to 1888 than had ever before been mined in one place. By itself the Sunshine Mine, the nation's largest silver mine, outproduced Nevada's famed Comstock Lode.

Washington's first gold strike came in 1854 on the upper Columbia at Fort Colville. Hundreds of miners trespassed on Yakama tribal land and some were killed. But the discovery of rich paydirt on Canada's Fraser River in 1857, and then in Idaho, lured miners to those richer areas.

When those rocks eroded, veins became accessible.

Very deep in the earth, magma discharges hot fluids that combine with groundwater that has penetrated cracks and faults. The superheated hydrothermal fluids rise by convection, dissolving and taking into the solution any minerals they encounter while circulating through dikes, sills, large intrusions, and zones of shattered, permeable rock.

They sometimes penetrate surrounding rock for more than a mile. As the fluid rises, temperature and pressure decrease so that minerals begin to precipitate out of the solution.

Since 1880, Oregon mines in the Blue Mountains, especially in Baker and Grant Counties, have yielded 70 percent of the state's gold and 74 percent of its silver. The huge Idaho Batholith is responsible for most of Idaho's ore deposits. Millions of dollars in gold probably still exists in the Boise Basin and along Idaho's upper Snake River, but that "flour" gold is too fine to concentrate. Today most gold is recovered as a by-product of refining other metals with which gold is associated, such as copper and silver. Despite the many large North Cascades batholiths, Washington never achieved the yield of Idaho and Oregon. (See All That Glitters)

MINERALS

Idaho is Mineral King of the Pacific Northwest. Most of its valuable mineral ores were found in the Coeur d'Alene mining district. Although Washington counts more than 30 minerals and ores, from antimony to zinc, located primarily in its northern counties, the majority of deposits are too small, of too low a grade, or too inaccessible for profitable mining. All three Northwest states have valuable supplies of sand and gravel, a legacy of ice-age glaciers, and diatomaceous earth, with Oregon one of the nation's top producers. Some deposits measure up to 100 feet thick and several miles long. At Idaho's City of Rocks lies one of the nation's largest deposits of diatomaceous earth. In eastern Washington the brilliantly white layers are sometimes found interbedded with dark lava.

Diatoms comprise most of the phytoplankton in fresh or salt water, a vital link in the food chain. The water in Oregon's Klamath Lake often turns green in summer with diatom "blooms" of the microscopic, one-celled algae. Since they reproduce by fission at least twice a day, trillions of them quickly accumulate. The tiny plants extract silica from water to form their elaborate, perforated hard cell walls. If the pinhead-

sized plants are not consumed by marine creatures, they die and sink to the ocean or pond floor. Some 5,000 species have been described, each with a distinctive shape of exquisite design: wheels, propellers, space stations, pill boxes. Diatoms are valued for gentle abrasiveness in toothpaste

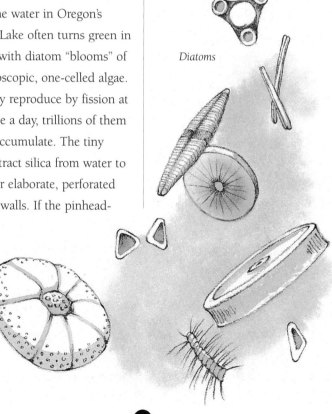

Diatoms

and silver polish and for resistance to chemicals and heat (1,000°F). Able to absorb 300 times their weight, they are used as filler in paint, brick, tile, and soap, as well as filters for wine, beer, and swimming pools.

Idaho's most valuable mineral, phosphate, is found in the huge Phosphoria basin. The mineral often occurs in rounded pebbles resembling black or dark brown limestone, although harder and readily taking a high polish. The best phosphate has weathered at great depths to a bluish white bloom. The richest beds, averaging 230 feet deep, are found in a waxy oil shale that burns, leaving an ash rich in copper, nickel, and chromium. The raw rock is used for slow-acting, long-lasting fertilizer. Phosphates are also used in explosives, industrial chemicals, sulfuric acid, detergents, and soft drinks. Idaho also produces mercury, gypsum, cobalt, and perlite.

PETRIFIED WOOD

Turning wood into gemstone requires no alchemist. Mineralization of wood preserved more than 200 species of trees in Washington's Ginkgo Petrified Forest State Park. The petrified remains of a ginkgo tree found in the area gave the park its name. Petrified ginkgoes are unknown elsewhere.

The state park contains more tree species than any other petrified forest in the world; 50 genera have been identified there, dating back 15 million years. They include hemlock, Douglas fir, crabapple, birch, myrtle, magnolia, cypress, chestnut, 8 of walnut, 9 species of oak, and 10 of maple. Included are a spruce 100 feet high and sequoias 10 feet in diameter.

Millions of years ago, this area was swampy lowland with small lakes and streams surrounded by forests. Trees fell from the hills into the mud of lakes, pools, and river deltas, and species from other regions floated down streams. About 17 million years ago, the great outpourings of basaltic lava began to flow across the Columbia Plateau, leveling the landscape, burning plants and trees. But these waterlogged, mud-covered trees wouldn't burn. The fiery lava, as it contacted cold water, formed pillow basalt that surrounded and protected the trees.

Buried wood usually decays, but when groundwater contains enough silica (picked up from volcanic ash) and other minerals, a slow replacement of wood by minerals occurs. Some wood remains, visible under a microscope, but most is replaced by silica as the groundwater percolates through openings in the wood. Wood becomes stone, with structural features such as growth rings and cell walls so

> **Washington's Ginkgo Petrified Forest State Park contains more tree species than any other petrified forest in the world.**
>
> ●

clearly visible in the agatized or opalized wood that identification of species is possible. Minerals or other compounds in the soil add brilliant color and patterns to the petrified wood. The layering process may not be so slow as once believed. Dead trees around hot springs in Yellowstone petrify quite rapidly.

SERPENTINE

Soft, weak, slippery, waxy. Strange words for a strange rock—serpentine. It is often associated with soapstone, also a serpentinite—a magnesium silicate that has absorbed water. Serpentine soil, lace with metals such as chromite, nickel, iron, and cobalt is toxic or stunting to plants.

Formed when peridotite, a rock of the earth's mantle, absorbs seawater, serpentine normally is found more than 3 miles below the basaltic ocean floor. But sometimes during mountain-building collisions between ocean and continental plates, serpentine slabs were preserved. Normally weak, serpentine often becomes very durable during mountain building.

The nation's most outstanding slab of exposed serpentine is a 2-million-year-old piece of ocean crust that stands nearly on edge in central Oregon's Canyon Mountain complex south of John Day Fossil Beds. Greenhorn Mountain in the northeastern corner of Grant County was named for a 300-foot-high monolith of greenish serpentine on Vinegar Butte. The rock is so slippery and so easily deformed it can work its way along faults and fractures and intrude into the center of another rock.

Attractively colored and sculpted examples of the rock are visible outside the southwestern Oregon town of Gold Beach. Normal bedrock in the Pacific Northwest is lava or granite, but occasionally serpentine appears as basement rock, providing a distinctive habitat for plant life. In Oregon's Siskiyous, chunks and larger masses of serpentine appear throughout faults and folds, hosting the second most diverse collection of plants in the nation. That soil is a potentially rich source of iron, nickel, cobalt, chromium, and talc.

"Serpentine barrens," where little vegetation grows, cause greenish and rusty red peaks south of Washington's Mount Stuart in the Wenatchee Mountains. Fidalgo Head and Cypress Island north of Deception Pass adjacent to the San Juan Islands abound in serpentine, toxic or stunting to most plants. (See Ice-Age Survivors; Blue and Wallowa Mountains)

FURTHER READING

Alt, David, and Donald W. Hyndman. Roadside
Geology of Washington. Missoula, Mont.:
Mountain Press, 1984.

———. Roadside Geology of Idaho. Missoula,
Mont.: Mountain Press, 1989.

———. Roadside Geology of Oregon. Missoula,
Mont.: Mountain Press, 1989.

———. Northwest Exposures, A Geologic Story
of the Northwest. Missoula, Mont.: Mountain
Press, 1995.

Angell, Tony, and Kenneth C. Balcomb III.
Marine Birds and Mammals of Puget Sound.
Seattle: University of Washington Press,
1982.

Arno, Stephen F. Northwest Trees. Seattle: The
Mountaineers, 1977.

Barcott, Bruce. The Measure of a Mountain:
Beauty and Terror on Mount Rainier. Seattle:
Sasquatch Books, 1997.

Beckwith, John A. Gem Minerals of Idaho.
Caldwell, Idaho: Caxton Printers, 1994.

Carson, Rob. Mount St. Helens: The Eruption and
the Recovery of a Volcano. Seattle: Sasquatch
Books, 1990.

Clark, Lewis J. Wild flowers of the Pacific
Northwest. Sidney, B.C.: Gray's Publishing,
1976.

Dietrich, William. Northwest Passage: The Great
Columbia River. Seattle: University of
Washington Press, 1996.

Gordon, David George. Field Guide to the Bald
Eagle. Seattle: Sasquatch Books, 1991.

———. Field Guide to the Slug. Seattle:
Sasquatch Books, 1994.

———. Field Guide to the Geoduck. Seattle:
Sasquatch Books, 1996.

Gordon, David George, and Chuck Flaherty.
Field Guide to the Orca. Seattle: Sasquatch
Books, 1990.

Halliday, William R. Caves of Washington.
Olympia, Wash.: Washington Department of
Conservation, Division of Mines and Geology,
1963.

Hare, Tony, ed. Habitats. New York: MacMillan,
1994.

Harris, Stephen L. Fire Mountains of the West:
The Cascade and Mono Lake Volcanoes.
Missoula, Mont.: Montana Press, 1988.

Kozloff, Eugene. Plants and Animals of the Pacific
Northwest. Seattle: University of Washington
Press, 1976.

Kruckeberg, Arthur R. The Natural History of
Puget Sound Country. Seattle: University of
Washington Press, 1991.

Mueller, Marge, and Ted Mueller. Fire, Faults &
Floods: A Road & Trail Guide Exploring the
Origins of the Columbia River Basin. Moscow,
Idaho: University of Idaho Press, 1997.

Nussbaum, Ronald A., Edmund D. Brodie Jr.,
and Robert M. Storm. Amphibians and
Reptiles of the Pacific Northwest. Moscow,
Idaho: University of Idaho Press, 1983.

Orr, Elizabeth L., and William N. Orr. Geology
of the Pacific Northwest. New York: McGraw
Hill, 1996.

Orr, Elizabeth, William N. Orr, and Ewart M.
Baldwin. A Geology of Oregon. 4th ed.
Dubuque, Iowa: Kendall-Hunt, 1992.

Ricketts, Edward F., and Jack Calvin. Between
Pacific Tides. 4th ed. Rev. by Joel W.
Hedgpeth. Stanford, Calif.: Stanford
University Press, 1968.

Scott, M. Douglas, and Suvi A. Scott. Heritage
From the Wild: Familiar Land and Sea
Mammals of the Northwest. Bozeman, Mont.:
Northwest Panorama, 1985.

Shaw, William T., John W. Aldrich, Stanley G.
Jewett, and Walter P. Taylor. Birds of
Washington State. Seattle: University of
Washington Press, 1952.

Slack, Adrian. Carnivorous Plants. Cambridge,
Mass.: Cambridge MIT Press, 1980.

Steward, Hilary. Cedar, Tree of Life to the
Northwest Indians. Seattle: University of
Washington Press, 1984.

Van Pelt, Robert. Champion Trees of Washington
State. Seattle: University of Washington
Press, 1997.

INDEX

ABOUT THE AUTHOR

Ann Saling has been writing about nature since 1972. For eight years she was a staff writer for *Pacific Search*, a monthly Northwest nature magazine. Her work has been published in *Woman's Day, Parents* magazine, *Organic Gardening, Northwest Travel, Ranger Rick,* and other publications. She currently teaches writing for the Creative Retirement Institute at Edmonds Community College.

After 22 years of traveling as a Navy wife—with Chile and Brazil her favorite duty stations—she now lives in Edmonds, Washington, with her husband, Fred. Her windows frame a view of Whidbey Island by day and the flashing light of Point No Point lighthouse at night. The beach and a panoramic view of the Olympic Mountains are a five-minute drive away.